Reaching for Your

New Life

Healthy Recovery from Divorce

Reaching for Your

New Life

Healthy Recovery from Divorce

Sara Rose, Ph.D.

VIP BOOKS

Visual Impressions Publishing

Reaching for Your New Life
Healthy Recovery from Divorce
©2010 by Sara Rose, Ph.D.

Cover photograph by Joe Gemignani/Joe Gemignani Photography
Cover and text design by Janet Aiossa/Adam Hill Design
Author photograph by Catherine Anderson/Catherine Anderson Studio

Published by:
Visual Impressions Publishing
10 Alexander Drive, Suite 633
Asheville, NC 28801
www.visualimpressionspublishing.com

From "At the Same Time" ©1987 Works of Heart Publishing
Used by permission – Ann Hampton Callaway

While the author has made every effort to provide accurate
telephone numbers and Internet addresses at the time of publication,
neither the publisher nor the author assumes any responsibility for errors
or for changes that occur after publication. Further, the publisher does not
have any control over and does not assume any responsibility for author
or third-party websites or their content.

ISBN-13: 978-0-9814633-4-6
ISBN-10: 0-9814633-4-7

Printed in the United States of America

Dedication

*This book is lovingly dedicated to
my two children, Charles and Louise,
who have always believed in me
and supported my efforts.
They have been wonderful teachers in my life
and I have learned so much from them.*

Acknowledgments

The road from formulating the idea of this story to completing it has been a long one. But I have been fortunate to have supportive people in my life during the journey of conception to completion and I want to gratefully acknowledge them.

I wish to thank both of my children for their loving acceptance of me and for encouraging me to write this book.

I specifically wish to thank my daughter and project manager, Louise Rose, for helping me bring this book to fruition through her insightful ideas and careful editing.

I also wish to thank my son, Charles Rose, for his many detailed and helpful suggestions about how to write and market my book.

I am very grateful to my good friend and mentor, Leah Berne for her support and encouragement.

I would like to thank my brother, Len Richardson; my cousin, Dr. Giles Floyd; and my friend, Dr. Kistler Osborne, for always supporting my efforts with kindness and caring.

I am grateful to Lowell Harris who always guided me through numerous computer problems.

I am grateful to Carson Weatherby for his creative suggestions for my book.

I wish to thank my publisher, Shelley Lieber, for her guidance and creative ideas for my manuscript.

I am thankful for all the rich experiences that I have had in my life and the people who have come into my life as my teachers and friends.

I will be forever grateful to all of my clients from whom I learned so much as they courageously began new journeys in their lives.

Disclaimer

Although the author and publisher have made every effort to insure the accuracy and completeness of information contained in this book, we assume no responsibility for errors, inaccuracies, omissions, or any inconsistency herein. The purpose of the book is to provide information that will inform and empower individuals during their transformation to a new, healthier life. However, as is the case with any book, it is general information and is no way designed to serve as or to take the place of professional advice or consultation with psychological or medical professionals regarding relationships, personal behavior, or the behavior or mental condition of any person.

Readers are urged to use the information in this book responsibly and appropriately. Because the actual implementation of the information is out of the author's and publisher's hands and is entirely up to the reader, the author and publisher can in no way take responsibility for any specific application of the information or for the results of its application. The reader is completely responsible for the application of this information and risks and results produced by its use. The author and publisher specifically disclaim responsibility for those risks and results.

If readers have any questions about their ability to be responsible and appropriate with the information presented in this book, they should consult an appropriate mental health professional before attempting to apply any of the information. If readers determine they are not able to use the information responsibly, they should not use it.

While all examples used in this book are taken from, and are faithful to actual occurrences, great care has been taken to protect the identity of all individuals. To this end, all identifying data have been substantially altered and many examples are mixtures of several different instances and individuals.

Contents

Introduction

As a counselor I have helped many courageous individuals whose stories are very powerful.

Throughout the book, you'll get snapshots of many different couples going through divorce. But we'll follow the complete journey of one woman: Claire.

Claire was a survivor who learned from her life experiences, and in doing so achieved acceptance, self-awareness, and a profound transformation. In each chapter, you'll see how with love, compassion, and unwavering determination, she wove the broken threads of her life back together again.

Part 1

Life Can Get Tangled

"Life is not the way
it's supposed to be,
it's the way it is.
The way you cope with it
is what makes the difference."

Virginia Satir

In the Beginning

In 1972, Claire's husband John was elected to the US Congress, catapulting their young family from a quiet existence in North Carolina to another world entirely—one of power, glamour, and glitz. Claire had been a stay-at-home mom, raising their young son Andrew while volunteering at church and in the community. She and John led normal lives, enjoying typical family pursuits, and were thinking about having another child. (After seven years, family members were impatient, asking when Andrew might have a little brother or sister.)

Although one of her husband's passions was politics, Claire never dreamed that he would actually run for office. But he did run, and when he won, her life—their lives—changed drastically.

Claire soon learned that a congressman's life is hectic. Her husband spent a great deal of time traveling back and forth between their homes in North Carolina and Washington, DC. When in Washington, he was expected to attend several events each night, many hosted by lobbyists. Claire would often accompany him to events, where they would speak with a few key people, and then move on to the next engagement.

Social events at the White House had them rubbing elbows with dignitaries and movie stars. Soon after their arrival in Washington, they were invited to the White House for a Sunday morning brunch featuring guest speaker Dr. Norman Vincent Peale. They met President and Mrs. Richard Nixon, and later were introduced to President Elect Jimmy Carter and his wife, Rosalynn.

With so many events to attend and the weather being so much colder in DC than it was in North Carolina, Claire found she had to expand her wardrobe. Although their social status had increased, their income hadn't kept up, and the cocktail dresses and evening gowns put a dent in her limited budget.

She often found herself feeling out of her comfort zone, both financially and socially. When President Carter's sister Ruth Stapleton passed away, Claire and John were invited to travel with the President and his wife on Air Force One to attend the funeral in North Carolina. She wondered: What were appropriate topics of conversation? What was the correct thing to wear? What was the proper way to board Air Force One? To deplane?

Although the President and First Lady had their own quarters onboard, Mrs. Carter spent a few minutes chatting with Claire. She was very gracious as they talked about their respective families. After landing, the President and First Lady exited first, followed by John, then Claire. They greeted the crowd at Pope Air Force Base, waving from the door of the plane, then walked down the steps of the plane across the tarmac. Claire just hoped she wouldn't trip.

Claire and her husband traveled frequently, both locally and abroad. On one trip to London, England, the congressional wives learned that they would be presented to Her Royal Highness Queen Elizabeth II. There were numerous matters of protocol to learn. Among other things, Claire was taught to curtsy. She was presented to the Queen and Prince Charles, who was much shorter than she had imagined.

Nine months after moving to Washington, Claire gave birth to a baby girl, Emily. She and John had wanted another child for a long time and they felt very blessed. A couple of years later, they had another little girl, Elizabeth. Their second daughter was born with a congenital heart problem, and they lost her after only two months. Claire was devastated.

During the last months of her last pregnancy, and during the brief time they had Elizabeth, Claire spent much of her time away from the social scene. She and John decided that it would be good for her to get out of the house and become involved in some of the same activities the other congressional wives enjoyed. To free up Claire's time, they hired a live-in housekeeper. Claire began attending meetings with the other congressional wives. She especially enjoyed The Congressional Club and was asked to chair the First Lady's Breakfast.

One of the most beneficial things that resulted from Claire's involvement with The Congressional Club was Miss Lillie's public speaking class. Miss Lillie, in her beautifully tailored suits and big hats, was an institution in the DC area. She taught Claire the mechanics of a good speech and how to relax in front of an audience. From that point forward, the ability to effectively and comfortably communicate with an audience served Claire well.

Things Change

Life was good. At least that's what Claire thought.

One night, she went to a concert and ran into some friends whom she hadn't seen in a while. She was looking forward to sharing their news with John. When she got home, he was watching television with the children, relaxing and having a great time.

After they tucked the children into bed, John told Claire that he wasn't happy. He said he had rented an apartment and was moving out the next day. He didn't give her any reasons.

Claire couldn't catch her breath. It was as if someone had kicked her in her stomach. Her first thought was, "This isn't really happening." All she could say, though, was, "Please don't go!"

He didn't answer and he made no promises. Like Scarlett O'Hara in *Gone with the Wind*, Claire thought, "I can't think about this anymore right now. I'll deal with this tomorrow." She thought he might change his mind in the morning. She didn't sleep at all that night. His words kept ringing in her ears.

The next morning John left for work as usual. Claire asked if he'd be back. He said he didn't know.

He never did come back home to stay.

Claire wondered, "How could my world, the world I have known for twenty years, be falling apart?"

She was numb. In the days that followed, she simply went through her normal routine. She told no one. The children didn't know what had happened. Their dad often traveled, sometimes for weeks at a time, so his absence seemed normal at first.

Claire cooked and cleaned. She took the children to their sports practices. She went to PTA meetings and Congressional Club activities. No one knew that anything was different.

Claire had thought her marriage was fine. She and John had promised to "love, honor, and cherish." She wondered: What gave him the right to abandon their relationship? To abandon their two children?

Even though she and John were often going in different directions and argued frequently, Claire didn't think anything was wrong. Wasn't that the price most people paid for leading busy, exciting lives? Just as she had been when she entered the glamorous life of a congressman's wife, Claire was caught unprepared.

Case Study

After enjoying four years together without children, Frank, a bank project manager, and his wife Shelly were ready for parenthood. But they weren't prepared for the changes that took place in their household when Daniel arrived. They were no longer free to come and go as a couple—something that they had taken for granted. To complicate matters for these new parents, the baby had colic for six months, and was awake many nights crying. Frank and Shelly were concerned about him, so they decided she should quit her job as curator of the local art museum to care for their son.

In time, the colic relented and Daniel was a healthy baby. Two years later, Frank and Shelly were ready to have another child, but it was eight years before Shelly got pregnant again and gave birth to their daughter, Sadie. When Shelly did not return to work, Frank felt pressure to make more money for the family. Having worked for the same company for many years, he had seniority. But when the company came under new management, Frank was expected to be more productive and work longer hours.

Frank had no time to help with this second child. Working long hours left him feeling unappreciated at work, irritable, and angry. Shelly—who had a lot on her plate with a new baby and a ten-year-old—didn't know what to do to help her husband. She and Frank no longer had time together: he left early in the morning and returned after she had fallen into bed, exhausted by the responsibilities of home and family. Since Frank was never home, Shelly met her emotional needs by doing things with their children.

She was so busy with the kids that she forgot that her husband also needed her attention. He became angry and very jealous of the children. He felt he was taken for granted not only at work, but also by his family. To Frank, it felt as if Shelly loved the children more than she loved him. She never took time to ask about how his work was going or offer to listen to any of his problems, he thought. Frank and Shelly became two strangers living in the same house.

One night Frank announced to Shelly that he couldn't take her coldness towards him anymore. He didn't feel that she cared about him. He wanted no more of her or the marriage, and he would build a new life for himself.

Shelly was stunned. She never dreamed that Frank was so unhappy. Although she begged Frank to try again or even go to marriage counseling, he refused.

There were many red flags that something was going wrong with Frank and Shelly's marriage: Frank isolating himself and not sharing, his anger with her, his resentment of the children taking her time. Yet he had never said a thing.

Happily married couples enjoy familiarity. They enjoy one another's company whether they're cleaning out the garage or going out to dinner. There are warning signs when a couple has stopped communicating: anger, sarcasm, irritability, or just being unavailable. These signs indicate someone is not feeling valued or appreciated. Every couple needs to work "together time" into their busy schedules. Without time alone, couples lack the closeness that a good relationship demands.

Emotional Fallout

Painful events in childhood can add to the pain of a soured relationship. Those who have felt that important people such as their mother and father were not there to help them feel loved, safe, and secure when they were young will feel the same terrifying fears when their partner leaves.

Fear of Abandonment

The fear of being completely alone or abandoned is one that is shared by many people. Children placed in foster homes may develop a fear that nobody wants them. The children of an alcoholic or drug addict might be handed to a grandmother to raise because their parents are unable to care for them properly. They may long for the day that the parent will come back. If someone has already had an experience of feeling abandoned in the early years, he or she may feel terrified and lost if a partner disappears.

For Claire, fears of abandonment surfaced when she and her husband separated.

As a baby, Claire could not digest her mother's milk and was taken to a children's hospital because she was not thriving. Her parents left her at the hospital, thinking that she would get the best of care and gain back the weight she had lost. When her parents came for a visit, Claire was screaming and she could not eat. Her parents took her home immediately and found a formula that she could tolerate.

The memory of being left in a strange place devoid of loving support became encoded in every cell of Claire's body in infancy. She had been afraid that no one would come back to get her. So when Claire's husband left, her experience was compounded because she had already felt abandoned as a baby. She would be all alone again—lost and without hope. Would she survive?

She wondered how she could be brave for her children when her heart was aching and she had no idea what the future held. John had been the breadwinner, and Claire had taken care of the household and the children. She hadn't worked outside the home in years. Claire asked herself, "What will happen to us now?"

Denial

Sometimes people facing divorce are overwhelmed by their emotions—they can't stop crying, they have bursts of rage, or they feel exhausted. Individuals who were not allowed to show their emotions while growing up—the "silent sufferers"—may hide their true feelings as adults. Feelings of panic are common, too, as well as fears of "going crazy."

There are feelings of detachment, numbness, and sometimes guilt. People try to pinpoint blame. "What did I do to cause this to happen?" These feelings can last for months. In some cases the spouse who has left will instruct the abandoned party not to tell anyone, and if that person is too dependent, he or she will stay quiet, never talking about the experience with anyone and never seeking much-needed help.

A person who has been left behind may fantasize: "If I wait, my spouse may reconsider." Many hope that what they are experiencing is nothing more than a bad dream. It is very easy to latch on to "what used to be," and all too terrifying to imagine "what is going to be."

Case Study

Judy and Sam, married for 30 years and parents of three children, felt that they knew each other's habits, preferences, and needs.

Sam, tall and lanky with graying hair, was president of his company. Judy, petite with deep blue eyes and blond hair, enjoyed her home, children, and friends. They loved to travel and had a second home at the beach. To outside observers, they seemed very happy.

At work, Sam relied on his administrative assistant, Jennifer, an attractive, energetic, young single woman. It was not uncommon for them to meet after office hours to plan upcoming events. She would often call him to update him on the latest news. While Sam traveled on business, they exchanged text messages. What once was strictly business communication came to include jokes and personal comments, as well as advice concerning her new boyfriend whom she really didn't care much about.

At the office, they joked, and their conversations grew more intimate and less businesslike. Sam was flattered by Jennifer's attention. One day, while Judy was out of town, Sam suggested to Jennifer that they hold a business meeting at his home.

Judy had gone to visit her sister, but became ill and decided to return home early. As she approached her driveway, she saw an unfamiliar car leaving. After parking her car in the garage, she found a wine bottle on the patio table and two wine glasses in the grass. Sam looked guilty as he tried to explain.

Judy knew she had interrupted something that had had little to do with her husband's business. She cried and demanded to know if Sam was having an affair. Even though Sam denied everything, Judy insisted they go to a marriage counselor. Sam agreed.

During the counseling sessions, Sam promised not to contact Jennifer again. He said that their marriage meant a great deal to him and he was willing to do his part. He seemed to be very remorseful and sorry that he had hurt his wife. Trust between the couple needed to be re-established because Judy had none now.

Sam continued to tell Judy that he had to work late. Then Judy unexpectedly found an email that indicated that Sam and Jennifer were planning to get a hotel room. At first, she thought there must be some mistake. In the marriage counseling session, Sam had agreed to work on their marriage. But his behavior remained the same. He was not telling her the truth. How could Sam do this to her after what he had promised?

Judy was angry and disappointed. Even though Sam said he wanted to be married to Judy, he continued to see Jennifer. Judy was in denial that her husband would want another woman and that he kept choosing to be with her. Her reasoning was, that if she denied it, she didn't have to deal with it, so it probably wasn't true. Her marriage just couldn't be over!

Some couples play emotional games with one another. Denying that there is a problem is a way to not get hurt or to just hold on.

A good relationship has no secrets. Trust is the cornerstone of marriage; without trust, a marriage disintegrates.

Experiencing Loss

Divorce leads to many kinds of losses, displacing the equilibrium in roles and relationships. Both spouses may feel that life is out of balance.

Loss of Identity

When a couple decides to divorce, both partners can experience a loss of identity. What once had been two partners in an intimate relationship with shared responsibilities becomes two individuals with different—and often expanded—roles and responsibilities.

One spouse may have been comfortable in the care-giving role, or relished the cache that came with being married. After divorce, that same spouse may acquire new financial responsibilities and have to leave the comfort of home to work. On the other hand, it may be that one partner now has greater responsibilities when it comes to disciplining children or creating a loving and nurturing home environment.

Loss of Support System

When one partner leaves, the one left behind not only loses the day-to-day support with household and child-rearing responsibilities, but also feels a loss of emotional support. Abandoned spouses feel as if they've been deserted by their "other half."

A parent going through a divorce has additional worries. Now there is only one adult in the home responsible for keeping everyone safe. If there are strange noises, one wonders if an intruder is breaking in. When a child develops a high fever in the middle of the night, there is no one to reassure the parent in charge that everything will be alright. Each partner has to perform dual roles, being both mom and dad.

Loss of Security in Relationships with Family and Friends

A newly single person may lose a sense of who he or she is with family members and friends. It can be awkward to be around them; to know what to say or whom to trust. There may be a sense that one is the focus of everyone's attention or pity, leading to feelings of sadness and self-consciousness that one is no longer the same person.

In encounters with friends, there may be awkward moments. Some friends don't know how to react to a single spouse when they were accustomed to interacting with a couple. There may be new alliances: one spouse will be invited to gatherings, while the other is not; one may receive advice and support while the other is avoided. The divorcing spouse may feel that he or she has lost friends.

Family members are sometimes harder to be around. They may want to be supportive, but not understand how they can be. They may feel awkward talking about your former spouse or grieving the loss of their relationship with him or her. They may offer advice without understanding the scope of the situation. It may be hard for them to understand how complicated the life of a divorcing spouse has become.

Loss of Road Map to the Future

Divorce means that plans for the future have been smashed: dreams of moving to a larger house, going back to school, having another child together, or going on a dream vacation are over. A mutual vision of a future together and a timeline as to when these events might happen has now been abandoned. That is all in the past now.

Divorcing spouses often wonder if there even is a future when it's not clear how to pay for next week's groceries, next month's mortgage, let alone next year's vacation.

Loss of Confidence and Pride

One of the biggest losses facing a newly single person is loss of confidence and pride. The one who has been left behind may ask: "What's wrong with me? What did I do wrong?"

Socially, both spouses may feel the pain of not being invited to events where the other will be present—the office holiday party, golf outings, or family gatherings. Even if invited, a spouse may no longer feel welcome at such events or not know how to face peers because of feelings of humiliation.

A newly single spouse may feel like a "nobody" who has been rejected, which can lead to feeling angry, defensive, and despondent. If one of the spouses is a high-ranking business person or a public figure, the media may report the separation, putting both people in the spotlight.

Case Study

Barbara, a fit and healthy fifty-year-old, had a personal trainer at her private club, enjoyed weekly manicures, and shopped often. She took her carefree lifestyle for granted.

At fifty-five, Doug, Barbara's husband, was an outgoing, handsome Ivy League university president. His work was demanding and included a lot of travel.

Barbara seldom asked her husband about his work at the university, nor did she express interest in his opinions or preferences.

Doug felt lonely, so when his work demands began to escalate, he added several evening business meetings to his schedule each week. He said that there was so much to do that he couldn't get it all done during the course of his normal work day and he could focus better at night.

Doug was given some tickets to a pro football game. Barbara didn't have any interest in sports, so he went alone. At the game, he struck up a conversation with the woman sitting two seats away. Her name was Janice, and she was an attractive energetic woman who loved football and life in general. She and Doug enjoyed the game and each other's company.

One weekend, Doug was working at home in his study, but his thoughts were of Janice. He emailed her to arrange a meeting later in the day. Doug was called away from his desk when the doorbell rang, leaving the email open. Barbara found the message and was shocked.

She confronted Doug and he told her that with Janice, he was happier than he'd ever been and he wanted a divorce.

Barbara always felt secure in her marriage. Now she had no way of changing Doug's mind.

As the weeks went by and the reality of Doug's leaving became clear to her, the once fit and pampered Barbara became depressed. She was exhausted and looked haggard. Those who knew her observed that she had changed from the confident wife of a university president to a lonely, angry woman.

Barbara's self-confidence had evaporated along with her self-worth and sense of identity. She didn't know who she was anymore, but she hated who she'd become.

Loss of Control

During a divorce, it's not uncommon to experience anger and resentment toward your former spouse or even at yourself. Anger might also be directed at God, family, or friends. It can be expressed in many ways and may escalate to uncontrollable wrath. A newly separated person may feel totally out of control while searching for a new identity.

Case Study

Natalie was an average looking, energetic thirty-eight-year-old woman with a high-stress job in customer service. Her husband Bert was the manager at a telephone company.

Bert had just turned forty and was balding. Forty seemed old to him. He was not happy and he discussed his problems with a co-worker, Flora. She always made time for him and seemed to understand him better than anyone else. He and Flora were drawn to each other and they made plans to live together. When Burt told Natalie about his affair and plans to leave, she was crushed. How could he do this to her?

Now Natalie not only had stress with her job but in her personal life too. Natalie had "temper tantrums" in which she cried, cursed, yelled, and screamed. She threw objects across the room. She was not only angry at her husband and Flora, but also with her friends, as well as her demanding job.

Her friends dared not disagree with her, because they knew she would get angry, raise her voice, and start screaming. They didn't enjoy her company anymore and so they avoided her.

Natalie was in pain and was unable to control her resentment. How dare Bert have an affair behind her back?

Loss of Health

There are physical symptoms related to grief. Loss of a love relationship can cause exhaustion, lack of sleep, and increases or decreases in appetite. Digestive problems and nausea are common. Frequent crying is another symptom. As emotions spill over, dizziness and lack of focus may occur. Headaches may develop as a result of the stress.

A suppressed immune system may lead to greater susceptibility to colds or the flu. Along with this, illness for longer periods of time is possible because the body is unable to defend itself against infection or disease.

Some experiencing divorce have trouble remembering something that just happened and have to ask people to repeat what they had just said. They may be irritable and fussy.

Case Study

Frances and Carter had been married for 18 years and they had three children. Frances was very happy and thought that her husband was happy, too.

When Carter told her that he was leaving, Frances's world crumbled. She became withdrawn and began experiencing migraine headaches. With these migraines, her eyes were very sensitive to light, so she was forced to go to bed and sleep. She tried to eat, but she couldn't keep anything down. She lost 15 pounds and had no energy.

Carter had always been responsible for chores as keeping the car in good running order, planning family vacations, and keeping the checkbook balanced. When faced with what had been her husband's responsibilities, Frances became nervous and anxious.

Frances got a job as a physician's assistant at a local doctor's office. However, she was frequently absent due to illness. With long hours at work and responsibilities at home, she was exhausted. It was as if she never caught up. She just wanted to stay in bed all the time.

After work, Frances felt too tired to help her children with their homework or ask how their day went at school. Instead she let the children watch television or talk on the phone, and bedtime was never enforced. Frances began getting calls from her children's teachers stating that they hadn't turned in their homework and they were falling behind in school.

Frances had difficulties focusing at work. She was often irritable and curt with patients, and they complained about her rudeness to her boss. She was warned that her behavior had to change or she would lose her job.

Because she was unable to handle the pressures resulting from her divorce and her different life, Frances found herself in jeopardy of losing her health, job, and even her children. Her boss suggested that she seek professional counseling to learn how to deal with her new responsibilities in a healthier manner.

Turning Loss into Gains

It takes time to develop the confidence to go on living. New circumstances can seem overwhelming. Part of learning to move on is learning who the "new you" is, and redefining the self. You will never be the same person you were when you lived with your spouse.

You are a new person.

Part II

Now What?

"You gain strength, courage, and confidence by every experience in which you really stop to look fear in the face. You are able to say to yourself, 'I lived through this horror. I can take the next thing that comes along.' You must do the thing you cannot do."

Eleanor Roosevelt

Facing Facts

Don't panic. Breathe. I know you are in shock. When your spouse says "goodbye," your life immediately changes. It is normal to feel insecure and panicky.

You may wonder—where will the money come from to buy everyday essentials such as food, medicine, gas? Who will pay the mortgage and the electric bill? Do you need a better job? Or, if you are not working, do you need to start searching for employment? Are you and your children still covered by insurance? Where are you going to live? Will the children have to change schools?

It is easy to become paralyzed by fear or overwhelmed by the enormity of what faces you. Resist these feelings. Accept that life will be different. But life hasn't ended. Yes, there are decisions that must be made. And you can make them. Focus on this thought: You can do it! You are a survivor.

Learning How to Prioritize

When you and your spouse decide to divorce, many things change. Sitting down and prioritizing the immediate things affecting your life right now is important.

Do not procrastinate! You must take time to sort out your priorities and then formulate a plan to act on them. By thoughtfully sifting through what has to be done first, next, and last, you will develop an action plan that allows you to get things done in a systematic way.

In Claire's case, she found herself easily overwhelmed. She began making lists of everything that she needed to do. For each item on her list, such as "get a job," she would list every step she could think of to accomplish that one thing; e.g., make calls, update her resume, find a career counselor.

You will have short-term, or immediate needs, and long-term goals. Recognize the difference between the two and focus on the immediate needs first. Sort your list by giving each item a priority level. Issues concerning your safety, health, legal, and financial well-being are your "A" priorities. List everything associated with achieving these "A" priorities and put them in order of how they can, or should, be accomplished.

You may need to move. If you stay in your current home, you may need to change the locks. List all the steps required to ensure your safety. Then begin working down your list. Cross things off the list as you achieve them. A list with many crossed-off items can be very empowering.

Because Claire wasn't working at the time of her divorce, she had a lot of time each day to work on what she needed to accomplish. However, if you are working, you may feel pressured or even overwhelmed as you try to find time to do even more.

Not everything is a simple matter of "just do it." Some issues are major life decisions. There are ways to cope with the decisions you must make. One method Claire used to clarify her decisions was to list on one side of a paper the "pros" of a particular choice, and on the other side list the "cons."

While debating whether to move or to stay put in Northern Virginia, on the "pros" side Claire listed:

1. This is the only home my children have known.
2. I know many people here now.
3. Our church is supportive.
4. The schools the children attend are superb.
5. Our medical support (doctors and dentists) is excellent.

On the "cons" side she listed:
1. Northern Virginia's cost of living is high.
2. Northern Virginia is very transient. Most of our neighbors have lived in the area for a short time and then relocated.
3. My mortgage is more than I can afford.
4. We have no family in the area.
5. I spend a lot of time in the car because of the distances to schools, children's activities, church, grocery store.

Eventually Claire decided to move back to North Carolina, where the cost of living was more affordable and family was closer.

When debating major decisions such as where to live, it is helpful to make a list as Claire did. Put all the positives on one side of the paper and all the negatives on the opposite side of the paper. Weigh the positives against the negatives, or observe which list is longer.

If you have more positive reasons to stay where you are, then think about how much rent or mortgage you are paying, and decide if you can afford it. If you decide you need to move, start thinking about how you will sell your home or if you can break your lease.

Identifying Your Needs

Some actions are too important to put off. While you may need time to accomplish many of the tasks on your list, take immediate steps to ensure your most urgent needs have been met.

Personal Safety

When Claire and her husband separated, she realized that she had never lived alone before. All of a sudden, she was solely responsible for the care of herself and her children.

One of the first issues to deal with was personal safety. Claire's fears made her conscious of every little noise in the house at night. She would awake terrified that an intruder was trying to get in. Claire's house had no security system, so the first thing she did was have an alarm system installed. She kept the code and emergency number on her bedside table.

Claire got to know her neighbors. A retired couple lived across the street. When she went back to work, this couple agreed to keep an eye on her home and watch for any unusual activity. It was a great comfort to Claire to know that this couple was willing to look out for her home.

Becoming familiar with her neighbors' habits gave Claire a feeling of security. She felt she would know when something out of the ordinary was happening, making it easier to know if and when she should call the police.

Claire also derived comfort from knowing that her community had a Neighborhood Watch group. When neighbors observed any strange activity, they called the police.

There are several ways that you can make your home safe. First, whether you rent, own your own home, or live in an apartment, make sure your home looks "lived in." Missing shingles or peeling paint suggest an unoccupied home. A well-kept yard or garden demonstrates that the occupant has interest in the home. A wreath on the front door welcomes friends.

Physical Safety

Claire and John had an equitable separation, but some couples are not so fortunate. Sometimes one partner is very angry and jealous and can become abusive. If this is your situation, develop a safety plan so you will be prepared to respond appropriately if you are physically threatened.

The National Coalition Against Domestic Violence (NCADV) offers the following suggestions:

If you are still in the relationship:
- Talk in a safe place: one with clearly marked exits and where weapons are prohibited
- Keep a list handy of people you can contact if your safety is threatened
- Always keep pocket change with you
- Memorize important numbers
- Initiate a "code word" or "sign" so that family, friends, co-workers will know when you need help
- Practice what you will say to your partner if he/she becomes violent

If you have already left the relationship:
- Get a new phone number
- Screen all your calls
- Be sure to save all contacts and messages and document injuries or other incidents involving your former partner
- Change the locks on your doors at home
- Do not stay alone
- Have a "get away" plan in case you are confronted by an angry ex-partner
- If you agree to a meeting with your ex-partner, do so in a public place
- Vary your routine
- Let contacts at school and work know what is going on
- Consider going to a shelter for battered women

If you are thinking of leaving a relationship, take important papers and documents with you to enable you to apply for benefits or take legal action. These documents would include your social security card, birth certificates for you and your children, your marriage license, leases or deeds in your name or both names, checkbook, charge cards, bank statements, insurance policies, medical records, and any record or police reports of past incidences of abuse. If you are going to a shelter, beware of taking any important information with you as it may be stolen. Instead, entrust those documents to a friend or family member.

Financial Safety
Identity theft is a threat to everyone, but may be more likely to happen when you are in a vulnerable position, such

as when you are going through a divorce. According to the FBI (Federal Bureau of Investigation), identity theft is the fastest-growing crime in the US.

People underestimate the resourcefulness of thieves who want money or need a stranger's ID. They can get private information from a variety of sources. They can retrieve your social security number or a pre-approved credit card application from the trash. They can steal your mail from a mailbox. Their antennae are up when you use your credit card in stores and restaurants.

To deter identity theft crimes, the Federal Trade Commission recommends:

- Shredding financial documents and paperwork with personal information before you discard them
- Keeping your social security card in a safe place (not your wallet) and avoiding writing your social security number on a check (give it out only if absolutely necessary or ask to use another identifier)
- Refraining from giving out personal information over the phone, through the mail, or over the Internet unless you know who you are dealing with
- Avoiding links sent in unsolicited emails. Instead, type in a web address you know. Use firewalls, anti-spyware, and anti-virus software to protect your home computer; keep them up to date
- Avoiding obvious passwords like your birthdate, your mother's maiden name, or the last four digits of your social security number
- Keeping your personal information in a secure place at home, especially if you have roommates, employ outside help, or are having work done in your house

It is important to monitor your financial accounts. If you are ever denied credit, find out why. React quickly if a business calls you about charges you didn't make. Get as much information as you can and look into it immediately. It may just be the result of simple error, but always check into it.

Legal Protection

Once you are safe and have a roof over your head, it is time to begin focusing on your legal situation. Develop a familiarity and understanding of legal terms and know your rights.

Typically, the first priority is to find an advocate to help you determine your rightful share of the marital assets. This person will help you prepare a separation agreement that spells out spousal support, division of property, health insurance, financial obligations, responsibility for debts, pension plans and retirement accounts, financial assets and tax returns, child visitation and custody of children as well as support. This is a critical decision because, of course, you want someone who will value you and your needs.

You must decide whether to hire an attorney or work with a mediator. When deciding how your assets will be divided—if both of you can be fair—it is much less expensive to work through a mediator. Sometimes (especially when there is little property to be divided) a mediator is the best solution.

Mediation

In divorce mediation, a couple negotiates a settlement themselves with the help of a mediator. The mediator is a trained facilitator who provides a safe atmosphere and leadership to help the spouses communicate in ways that they probably would not be able to due to the strained nature of the relationship. The mediator's job is to help each partner negotiate issues such as alimony, child support, and how their property will be distributed. Handling a straightforward divorce usually requires four to twelve sessions.

Even if you use a mediator for your divorce settlement, you can still hire a lawyer to advise you and support you in the separation process. This is not absolutely necessary, but gives you a legal opinion to determine your rights and options. Your lawyer will not attend the mediation sessions.

The advantages of using mediation include:
- Lower cost
- Speedier process
- Amicable agreement is more likely
- Better communication

Mediation is for responsible adults. It is a process in which a couple negotiates with one another in good faith. It will not work well if one spouse is unable to make sound decisions due to severe emotional problems, learning disability, or drug or alcohol addiction.

Once the separation agreement is signed, it is a legal document and outlines the assets you will have when beginning your new life. Your separation agreement determines alimony and how assets are split. If there are any children, the agreement will also specify child support and custody arrangements. If either party breaches the agreement in any manner, legal action may result.

If you and your spouse cannot work with a mediator to determine a fair settlement of assets, then you will need to hire an attorney. Your lawyer is responsible for negotiating what is best for you.

Case Study

One night after a big argument, Kevin told his wife Deidra that he was not happy with their marriage and that he was leaving her and the children. He had already packed his clothes, and walked out without even saying goodbye.

For weeks, Deidra begged her husband to come home. She tried emailing and text messaging. He responded occasionally, until finally, he completely ignored her desperate messages.

She finally realized that her husband was serious. Because she was not employed and had no income of her own, she was hesitant to hire an attorney.

The only attorney she knew was her father-in-law. She believed that someone in his firm would fairly represent her interests. She was wrong.

Deidra ended up with no alimony and no child support. The lawyer she chose was her father-in-law's partner in the law firm. His loyalty was with his partner and his partner's son. Deidra realized too late that she was now entirely responsible for making decisions concerning her own best interests.

How to Choose a Divorce Attorney

Because your attorney is responsible for determining what your lifestyle will be for the foreseeable future, learn how to discern who can give you the best representation.

• Choose someone in the field of divorce law
• Select a lawyer with up-to-date certification
• Find someone who will represent your best interests

When beginning your search for a lawyer, ask people you know who are divorced if they can recommend a lawyer for you. If you don't know anyone who is divorced, then ask family members, friends, or people at work if they know someone who can recommend a divorce attorney. When asking for referrals, find out which lawyers are capable as well as which to avoid.

Sometimes women choose to work with women lawyers, and men sometimes prefer men. You might feel that an attorney of your gender would be in a better position to empathize with your issues. In fact, he or she may have gone through a similar experience. However, never choose a lawyer on gender alone. Hire a lawyer based on his or her skills.

Before deciding if a lawyer is right for you, ask for a free consultation. This is an opportunity to determine if this professional understands your particular issues. Discuss what you want from the divorce and ask the lawyer to honestly evaluate your situation for you. In asking for a free consultation, you can decide if this particular lawyer is a good fit for you without incurring any expense.

There are many ways to obtain information regarding

lawyers. The Internet is a great resource when you're looking for information about divorce lawyers and their credentials. You can search online for information about your local bar association, the professional organization to which lawyers belong. There you can find local attorneys who specialize in divorce law.

There is an American Bar Association, too, but not every lawyer belongs to that organization. State bar associations have the most power over their members because the group decides who can practice law in each state. The state bar can also discipline or disbar members. If you choose to call your state bar association, find out if your state has a specialist certification for divorce lawyers.

Just as certain judges hear traffic violations, certain judges hear divorce cases in their courtrooms. You can find out when the judge will be holding hearings by calling his or her clerk. Visit the courtroom and watch how various lawyers work. Ask the clerk or bailiff to give you the names of those attorneys who seem most competent and best suited to represent you.

Collaborative Family Law

Collaborative family law (established in 1991) is a relatively new way of settling divorces. It began in Minneapolis, Minnesota, when a small group of lawyers decided to try to "do something different." They had such positive feedback from their clients that the concept took hold and grew.

Often, in a traditional court setting, each spouse's lawyer fights to get the biggest "piece of the pie" for his or her client, often eliciting intense emotional responses such as anger, resentment, even hatred.

The cooperative approach allows divorcing spouses to negotiate and settle their issues with a lawyer without going to court.

Each spouse selects a lawyer from a group that practices collaborative law. The couple and their attorneys agree to resolve all issues without court proceedings. The couple's issues are negotiated in a controlled and safe setting, in an environment that is less formal and less threatening than court. This highly individualized technique allows the team to develop an agreement that will work for each particular family.

During the meetings, spouses explore their issues and voice their concerns. The lawyers act as negotiation coaches for their clients, advising them about their entitlements and obligations. Threats and/or offensive comments are not tolerated. The lawyers focus solely on reaching a settlement.

Participants in the collaborative law team vary depending on each family's needs. In addition to the couple and their attorneys, mental health or financial-planning professionals are sometimes involved.

The collaborative process is generally less expensive than going to court. Realize, however, that highly trained professionals charge accordingly. Their time will not be preparing documents for court, but rather managing negotiations, keeping you focused on your needs and wants, reviewing your legal rights, and crafting an acceptable agreement. This process moves faster because it does not rely on the court's calendar.

Getting to Solid Ground

Sometimes less urgent, but equally important, is your need for a stable life. Basics such as shelter and income will help you feel like you are moving on to solid ground.

Shelter

Shelter ranks among your top needs. You need to determine what you can afford. If you have children, your new living quarters might be determined by the schools your children would attend and the neighborhood where you'd like them to be raised.

If a couple owns a home together, one of the first questions that arises when they separate is: Who gets the house? If the house has a mortgage, who is responsible for making the payments? The couple has the option of selling the property, but that means new living quarters for everyone involved.

When Claire's husband left, he moved into a nearby apartment; she and the children stayed in the house. Claire knew that they would be financially unable to stay there permanently. She contacted a real estate agent and the house went on the market. It took two years before the house was sold. During that time, it was Claire's responsibility to pay the mortgage.

Finances

Another priority is coming to terms with your new financial situation.

When your marriage breaks up, you may be surprised to discover that your bank accounts are depleted of money—money that you might have been counting on. If your spouse is moving out, immediately check your joint bank accounts. Angry or bitter spouses often try to make it very hard for their former partners to get started with a new life. If you have a safety deposit box, familiarize yourself with its contents. Periodically open it and examine the documents inside to be sure that they are up to date.

If your spouse closes out your joint account, then he or she may use money as a bargaining chip or take all the money and hide part of it.

Determining how much money you have will dictate not only where you live, but how you live. Odds are great that you will be living on less money than when you were married, and your expenses must keep pace with your adjusted income.

You may need to readjust your spending habits. Can you afford to drive the kind of car that you currently have? If you have children, do you need to forego private schools and transfer to public schools? Can you afford to dine out?

Living within a budget is a matter of making wise choices and using self-discipline. Know the amount of money coming in every month and deduct the amount required for the necessary expenses, such as your mortgage or rent, health insurance, food, and your utilities. If you have any money remaining, decide whether to spend it or invest it.

You should strive to keep a good credit record, which means paying your bills on time and resisting the urge to overspend. Learn to be flexible and prepared for the unexpected, because sometimes the best laid plans fall apart.

Claire and her children had been dependent on John's income while Claire kept the household running and was responsible for their children. When they first separated, she didn't know where to begin or how to pick up the pieces of her life and move on.

If, like Claire, you've relied on your spouse to manage your finances, you may need to acquire some money management skills of your own. Find someone you trust, or seek professional help. Most banks have someone who can meet with you.

If you have money invested in stocks, bonds, or mutual funds, meet with a financial advisor and discuss your portfolio. Learn how and why your money is invested as it is. It may be time to make changes.

The liquidation of any assets during your divorce can affect tax filings. Therefore, it is also important to meet with your tax preparer to ensure that your finances are in order as far as the IRS is concerned.

Case Study

Ann was never good at staying within a budget. As a college student, when she ran out of money, her parents always bailed her out, sending whatever amount she needed. Consequently, she never worried about money and she never learned the skill of money management.

She finished college and found a job, but never planned how she would spend her paycheck. Sometimes her money ran out before the end of the month. Creditors began calling, but still she resisted learning how to manage money.

When Ann married, she continued her reckless ways. Her husband, on the other hand, was very careful with his money. The two never agreed when it came to financial matters.

After her marriage failed, Ann still had no idea how to manage money. Her sister, however, had always lived within her means. Ann asked her sister to teach her the principles of money management. Although it was difficult for Ann at first, she learned how to live within a realistic budget, thanks to her sister's patience and guidance.

Here are some steps you can take to learn to live within your budget:

- Analyze your personal values regarding money
- Evaluate your needs and what they cost
- Keep a record of what you buy and how much you spend
- Evaluate your spending habits
- Learn how to save
- Keep only one credit card and pay the balance every month
- Use rebates and clip coupons

- Pay a little extra monthly toward the principal on your mortgage
- Rent if you can't afford to buy a house
- Buy used items
- Comparison shop when buying large items
- Use generic brands
- Pay cash
- Join a mother's group with children the same age as yours and take turns babysitting
- Encourage older children to get part-time jobs

Employment

If you already have a job, you are fortunate because you are bringing in some income and may have insurance benefits. However, if you need to find a better job or earn additional income, there are many ways to do so.

If you're in the market for a job, go online and visit a variety of employment sites. Many sites help narrow your job choices and often there is a way to create and then post your resume online. You're not guaranteed to find a job this way, but you will get an idea about the kind of jobs that are available. Be wary of sites that ask for payment before they help you locate employment.

Here are four key steps when looking for employment via the Internet:

1. Use specific key words to search for a job
2. Develop an up-to-date, detailed resume
3. Be patient—the process takes time
4. Always respond promptly to calls or emails from prospective employers

If you are unsure about what type of job you want, consider meeting with a career counselor. A career counselor is required to have a master's degree in a field such as mental health counseling, and must be licensed. These counselors help people evaluate their interests and their abilities, usually by administering a battery of tests.

Once likely career options have been identified, your counselor will recommend strategies for reaching your career goals. If you live near a college, find out if the school offers career testing that can help you determine the jobs for which you are best suited.

Another option is to find a life coach. These coaches are trained to listen to your dreams and goals and support you throughout the process of meeting your objectives.

When Claire and her husband separated, she had no idea how she was going to support herself and her children. Claire's teaching certificate had expired, so she couldn't teach in Virginia. She had been a stay-at-home mom for more than twelve years. She had not gone for a job interview in 15 years. "What should I wear? What should I say?" she thought. Claire was terrified! However, her desperate need of a job spurred her on.

She asked her ex-husband to help her find a temporary job. When he gave her the name of someone at the Central Intelligence Agency (CIA), she just laughed. What could she possibly do for the CIA?

But, she made the call and went for an interview. She was offered and accepted a secretarial position in the CIA's Public Affairs Office, which was near her home and daughter's school.

This job served her well for two years. The position made

it possible to keep a roof over her head and food on the table, but she knew that it was only temporary while she determined whether it was better to stay in the DC area or to move.

Through a career counselor, Claire took a series of tests that told her that she would be good working with people, possibly in teaching or counseling. Claire knew that she did not want to teach again. While she loved teaching and the interaction with children, the paperwork was not her cup of tea.

After she moved back to North Carolina, Claire met with another career counselor who helped her re-acclimate to the area. This counselor looked at the results of Claire's Virginia test scores and suggested she consider getting a master's degree in counseling. Claire learned that her local constituent institution of the University of North Carolina system had an excellent counseling program.

Claire took courses for two years before she earned a master's in counseling. She interned at a local hospital and by the time she had completed her nine-month internship, Claire knew that she had found her calling. Less than two years later, she was offered a full-time counseling position at the hospital where she'd completed her internship—her dream job at the time.

Picking Up the Pieces

Once your basic needs are met, you will have to face the more complicated task of confronting your emotions.

Confronting Resentment and Other Negative Emotions

Immediately following the breakup of your marriage, you may feel you have little or no control over life-changing events. You may find it very difficult to deal with your resentment during this period of adjustment.

You may feel that you are being treated unfairly or plagued with doubts: what if you can't do all that is suddenly required of you?

Negative emotions—anger, resentment, bitterness, regret, and shame—can consume you and keep you from moving forward.

Grief

The loss you experience due to divorce is similar to what you experience when a loved one dies. Some sort of grieving process is necessary. The transition of moving through being unhappy and miserable to reaching recovery can be painful and unpredictable. Research indicates that it takes the average person about two to five years to fully recover from divorce.

Allowing yourself to grieve the loss of love, security, and your marriage is necessary. Not taking the time to grieve keeps you from being able to move forward and begin the next chapter in your life.

Case Study

Karen and Robert had been married for 25 years. Their children were grown and married with children of their own. Robert was approaching retirement from a long career in county government, and was looking forward to doing things that he had never taken time to do when he worked. He had always said that when he retired they'd spend a week or two at the beach, or visit New England when the leaves turned.

A year before Robert retired, a young divorcée began working at his office. They would chat, and before long she began asking for advice about problems she was having being a single mom. At first, all he wanted to do was help. Soon, Robert found himself enjoying their friendship immensely. He looked forward to talking with her every day and soon just the sound of her voice made him happy.

One weekend, he told Karen he was going away on business, but he actually went away with his co-worker. Later, he left the marriage.

Karen felt cheated and humiliated. She could not face the fact that Robert was never coming back home. All the plans that they had made together had been abandoned.

Karen got busy so she wouldn't have to think about losing her husband. She volunteered to keep the grand-children. She went on trips with the local senior center. She volunteered for several jobs at her church. She went out for dinner nearly every night, then came home and fell into bed exhausted. Karen plunged headlong into all this activity so that she didn't have to deal with her new life...a life without her husband.

Stages of Grief

Dr. Elizabeth Kubler-Ross identified the stages of grieving as: denial, anger, bargaining, depression, and acceptance. These emotional milestones do not always occur in the same order, but provide some guidelines to follow as you heal emotionally.

Denial

The initial period of grief is punctuated by shock, disbelief, and denial. There are thoughts such as, "I can't believe this is happening to me!" Denial means you're not facing the reality of what is happening. This stage may last for hours or weeks. You may experience feelings of numbness or almost feel paralyzed because you are not ready to deal with the truth. Your body will try to protect you from reality. Sometimes, when there is a knock on the door, or the phone rings, your heart may soar because you are sure that it is your spouse returning. You may imagine that you see him or her in traffic or walking down the street.

Accepting the fact that your spouse is not coming back is very difficult. A husband may rationalize that his wife will get over the other man, or think that her affair is just a "fling." He may try to keep everything in the house just as it was when they lived together. He may tell himself that if he just hangs in there long enough, his wife will surely realize what a remarkable man he is and return.

Another way to deny loss is to deny the meaning, or depth of the loss. An abandoned spouse may tell others that she and her husband were never that close anyway, or that she doesn't really miss him. Playing down the significance of the loss by removing anything that evokes old memories also renders the loss less crippling.

Loss must be accepted both on an intellectual level and on an emotional one. Acceptance of the loss of a loved one takes time. The many rituals that couples establish in their lives together—special things they do at birthdays, anniversaries, or during the holidays—must be replaced; new paths have to be forged.

Case Study

Margaret could not believe that Tony, her husband of 30 years, had left to be with another woman half her age. Margaret was beautiful, talented, and had much to offer. After Tony moved, he left behind his favorite chair, a few pieces of clothing, and mementos from their travels together. Margaret didn't want reminders of their life together. She threw out all of Tony's belongings, and anything else that reminded her of him. To further minimize her loss, she eventually moved to another house. She didn't feel as humiliated when she wasn't confronted by things that they shared. Without the vestiges of her old life, she didn't have to face the fact that her husband was happier with a younger woman and she was the one left behind with only old memories.

Anger

The next stage of the grieving process as defined by Kubler-Ross is anger, a normal response to any type of suffering. When you realize that there is nothing you can do to make a spouse come back, you can become angry and full of rage.

Anger can also manifest itself as a regressive experience when you lose someone you love. It is painful to be rejected.

You are hurt and have no control over the situation, so you may lash out like a toddler separated from his mother while shopping. The child punches her when reunited. His anger is addressing the panicked feeling he had while alone. His punch really meant, "Don't leave me again!"

Anger seeks an outlet, and it takes diverse forms to do so. It can be felt as resentment, hatred, accusation, or a sense of unfairness. Underneath these strong emotions is a deep sadness which is recognition that getting back together is not likely to happen.

Anger can be directed at anyone—family members, children, God, the former spouse or lover, or even oneself. Anger can also take the form of general irritability or frequent outbursts. Individuals can speculate "if only" they had done something differently, the loved one would not have left. Therefore, the person left behind uses anger as a fruitless effort to restore the relationship.

There can also be hostility and ingratitude toward friends who try to nurture the person who has experienced a loss. Often people don't want comfort for the loss, but assistance toward reunion.

Bargaining

You might find yourself thinking or saying, "I'd do anything if only my partner would come back." You may promise to change, to never complain again, to move, to put up with occasional straying—anything. You may bargain with yourself, with God, with the person who has left.

If you hear that he or she will even consider returning, you have a glimmer of hope. But this can be false hope.

Do not trade yourself away in the form of money, dignity, your self-esteem, or even your faith when you are in the desperate stage of bargaining. You could be in danger of making mistakes that may impede your success in the future.

Bargaining tactics seldom save a relationship; they only rob the traders of their dignity. You have no control over another person's wishes, no matter how much you may change.

When you have reached the bargaining stage, you are no longer in denial; you realize that the relationship could end. Sometimes a couple may choose to try again. But if an unhealthy relationship has been allowed to continue too long, established, unhealthy patterns continue. Problems are not identified and solved, and many times one or both of the partners are miserable. The relationship will continue as before, unless the couple is willing to learn to identify the problems that ruined the relationship and employ constructive ways to solve those problems.

Depression

Depression, a normal part of loss, can occur during any of the stages of grief. Depression seems to be even more pronounced if a divorcing couple has been together for a long time and invested a great deal in their marriage. When two people have bought a home together, had children, and been active in their community, they have invested a lot of emotional, spiritual, and financial effort. When this lifestyle ends, they ask, "Who am I now, without my partner?" Feelings of hopelessness and emptiness can last for months, or even years.

Claire did not realize how hopeless and depressed she

felt in her marriage until after her husband left. She realized, in hindsight, it would have been far better if she had acknowledged and accepted her true feelings, rather than shutting herself off and becoming numb.

After her marriage, Claire was so busy trying to somehow make the pieces of her life fit together that she ignored her feelings. She simply stuffed them down inside. That was a mistake. She could have more easily come to terms with the dissolution of her marriage had she acknowledged how she felt and let herself experience the pain.

If you can accept that it is normal to feel sad, lonely, depressed, or lost, then you have begun the healing process. It is important to let yourself feel any negative feelings so you can move on with your life.

The following are some common symptoms of depression:

- Feeling physically and emotionally drained
- Experiencing a lack of appetite or, conversely, eating all the time
- Getting sick frequently
- Crying all the time
- Inability to cry at all and keeping feelings inside
- Feeling guilty and criticizing yourself: "If only I had..."
- Lack of energy
- Inability to sleep
- Loss of interest in life, work, home
- Periods of extreme hopelessness and helplessness
- Fantasizing about the past
- Drinking too much
- Using drugs inappropriately

If you find that you are feeling increasingly worse, go to your family physician, or see a psychiatrist. You can ask for an antidepressant until you are better able to handle your grief. Though everyone grieves differently, on average, six months of taking antidepressants is sufficient. You will know it's time to stop when you are feeling stronger. A common misconception is that you will be yourself in a week or two. It is important to give yourself time to move forward.

Even though valuable support can be derived from self-help groups or other small group interaction, many people complain of a deeper level of sadness, an emotional loneliness. Emotional loneliness occurs when there is no involvement in a committed relationship.

In a committed relationship, you have agreed to be exclusively with one person. The relationship fosters expectations of fidelity, commitment, and love from that person that lead to a feeling of security for both parties. You look forward to your loved one's coming home for supper, going places with you, or sharing your heartfelt hopes and dreams.

When a couple decides to go their separate ways, the emotional support is shattered, and the resulting hopelessness and loneliness can be unbearable.

You may choose to seek counseling from a licensed counselor or psychologist. These individuals are trained to help those grieving due to the loss of a relationship. The sessions are always confidential. The counselor should be objective and suggest resources to help with the healing process. Counseling can help you become healthier and gain confidence in your ability to cope with life and move forward.

On those days when nothing goes right, you need someone with whom you can share your deepest thoughts. It can be a relative or trusted friend; someone who will accept you just as you are and be a good listener.

It would have helped Claire to have someone to confide in, but she had too much pride to tell anyone how much she was suffering. She believed that others saw her as someone who "had her life together." How could she let them see that all of her confidence was gone, that she didn't know where she was going to live, or even who she wanted to be? Claire kept to herself and cried a lot. It never occurred to her that she might be depressed.

Even though you feel exhausted and it is painful to deal with the difficulties in your life, beware of abusing drugs or drinking too much. The relief that you may get from these is short-lived; the next day you will still be faced with the same problems. It is frighteningly easy to start depending on chemical substances to boost your confidence, especially if there is any family history of addictive behavior. You do not need the problem of addiction added to the many challenges you are facing.

Acceptance

When you have worked through the other stages of grief, you arrive at the last stage: acceptance. You now realize that your partner is not coming back; your marriage has ended. You accept the fact that now you have to get on with your new life.

If you have spent time working through your grief in a healthy way and have worked on yourself, then possibly you have learned how to have a healthier life than you ever had before. You may even realize that having an unhappy marriage end is the best thing that ever happened to you.

Beyond Grief: Love Addiction

When a relationship ends, it is a struggle to cope with the absence of a partner. With extreme loss, there is an accompanying chemical withdrawal. Some people have an especially difficult time processing changes in their relationships and seem to be more adversely affected by the chemical changes in their brains. Their inability to move on can have unfortunate, and sometimes extreme, consequences.

You've probably read stories of men and women who await trial or are serving jail sentences for attempted kidnapping, battery, assault, and even murder of their former spouses. Some claim temporary insanity or cite obsessive-compulsive disorder, depression, insomnia, or psychotic disorders.

Helen Fisher, PhD, an anthropologist at Rutgers University, conducted research that supports the fact that love can be addictive. She applied brain-imaging technology to volunteers who looked at pictures of their romantic partners. The areas of their brains that responded were the same areas that responded in drug addicts' brains when confronted with their high of choice.

She looked at the properties of infatuation and found that they had some of the same elements as a cocaine high: sleeplessness, loss of a sense of time, and an absolute focus on love, to the detriment of everything else. Her research also revealed that infatuation can overrule more rational brain functions.

Brenda Schaeffer, author of *Is It Love or Is It Addiction?*, acknowledges that all addictions—whether they be related to drugs, alcohol, food, gambling, smoking, or love—affect the arousal, fantasy, and satiation neuropathways in the brain. Some individuals may even experience withdrawal symptoms when a relationship comes to a halt. They long for the "high," or rush, that occurs when their lovers are present.

A chemical in the brain called phenylethylamine (PEA) is involved with the euphoria that individuals experience when they fall in love. This chemical rises in the brain when you experience feelings of infatuation, which elevates levels of euphoria and excitement. Thoughts such as "this is the only person for me" trigger the arousal. If you carry memories of when your relationship was at its height, these thoughts continue round and round on a loop in your brain. The fantasy feeds the addiction.

The best way to break this cycle is to modify your thoughts and cease to fuel the addiction with fantasy scenarios that are no longer your reality.

The following are suggestions that will help you move on from the past and focus on the future:

- Be aware of your love-addiction tendencies (obsessive thoughts about the other person that interfere with your life, feelings of worthlessness and depression when not in a relationship)
- Learn how to identify healthy love and know that it does exist
- Accept the loss and resist the pain that letting go produces
- Discover the underlying causes and psychological beliefs that support your obsessive behavior

Questions to ask yourself:

- Why do I fear closeness?
- What do I believe about relationships, love, and myself?
- Do I believe that people will disappoint me or that I will disappoint them?

In addition to asking yourself these questions, focus on the following tasks:

- Release the past and focus on having success in future relationships.
- Find a therapist trained in love addiction or a support group such as Sex and Love Addicts Anonymous.

Moving Beyond a Co-Dependent Relationship

People in co-dependent relationships are willing to do anything to please their spouse, even if they hurt themselves.

People will endure verbal and mental abuse, sometimes even physical abuse, because they have learned from childhood that how they are treated doesn't matter.

Individuals who have been treated badly by either or both parents have a tenacious, instinctual, compulsive need to connect with the parent. They believe that without this connection to the parent, they will not survive. As adults, these people often repeat this behavior with their spouses.

Women primarily value connection. It's important to them and they long for it. When their connection is broken with a man, it is agonizingly painful.

This need for connection is also found in nature as illustrated by the relationship between the yucca cactus and the yucca moth. The yucca plant grows in the Midwest, and every spring sprouts a tall stalk of white flowers, where the little white yucca moth lives.

The yucca moth is dependent on the yucca plant. There are no other plants that can sustain the yucca moth's survival. The yucca caterpillars must eat the yucca seeds or they will starve. The moths would die without the plant. The opposite is also true: The plant would die without the moths to help it reproduce. So their relationship is symbiotic—totally dependent.

One could say the yucca moth has a blurred sense of self. It will not seek other plants to pollinate, only the yucca plant.

Case Study

Connie and Jack had three children. Jack had a prestigious job as a vice-president in a large corporation. She felt she was being a good wife when she did things that made him happy. He chose when they would have sex. He controlled their finances, told her what social events they would attend, and what to wear. He chose the schools their children attended. When Connie tried to speak up, Jack would have a temper tantrum and yell and scream in anger. He withheld credit cards. His behavior was getting out of control.

Connie wondered how their relationship got off

track. She thought she was being a good wife by doing everything his way, but after awhile Jack's behavior left her frustrated and exhausted. Jack's perception of marriage was that husbands "keep their wives in line." He refused to see that there was any problem. Jack couldn't comprehend why Connie asked for a divorce.

In a relationship, you trust your partner to respect your feelings. When you are with a controlling personality or someone who puts you down in everything you do, the trust is destroyed along with your self-esteem. You don't like yourself and you become angry at your loved one. This can lead to separation and divorce.

Many women have a blurred sense of who they are. They are caught in the belief that they are only what their father, mother, boyfriend, or husband says they are. They lose themselves in someone else. But unlike the yucca moth—which is biologically bound to the yucca plant—women have choices.

Case Study

Fran was an eleven-year-old ward of the state. Her parents divorced because her father was an alcoholic and frequently beat her mother, who was a prostitute.

Sometimes, when her father was in a drunken rage, he beat Fran, too.

A social worker, counselor, and medical doctor were assigned to help Fran. At her court hearing they made recommendations to the judge that she be placed in foster care.

The judge leaned forward and asked Fran where she would like to live. Fran responded immediately that she wanted to go back home and live with her father. Fran had a longing for love even to the point of going back home to a destructive, abusive parent who could never love her.

An example of how important attachment is for living beings is illustrated by Konrad Lorenz, an Austrian animal psychologist, who was awarded the Nobel Prize for Medicine and Psychology in 1973 for his study of imprinting in animal behavior. His work proved that there are important periods in life when definite stimuli are necessary for normal development. He conducted research in which he demonstrated that goslings could be imprinted not only to human beings, but also to objects such as a white ball or a toy duck. He found that after hatching, goslings will follow and become attached to the first moving object they see. Usually this is their mother duck. If Lorenz were present when the goslings were hatched, they followed him around as if he were their parent.

If a father spends little time with his daughter or doesn't engage while they are together, the girl will develop little, if any, self-worth. He may tell her to "go play" while he watches TV or uses the computer. She may feel invisible and unworthy of his attention. Every time he criticizes her, it only reaffirms her belief that she is unworthy. She will try over and over to get his approval. If he tells her that she is fat, she will attempt to lose weight, even to the point of becoming bulimic and endangering her health, just to please him. Even if she is an excellent student, she will redo her work over and over, becoming a perfectionist in order to be "good enough."

This little girl desperately tries everything she can to be accepted and loved. But no matter how hard she tries, she never gets the acceptance and love from her father that she yearns for. When she grows up, she still believes that if she tries harder and harder she will finally get the love she so deserves. Of course this never happens, and she is left feeling empty. This is co-dependent, or people-pleasing, behavior.

Because co-dependent women compulsively try to please (it could be her boss or husband), they have no sense of who they are. They try to be the women they think the men in their lives want them to be.

Taking Positive Steps to Physical and Emotional Health

Creating a new life is hard work. Take each new step one day at a time. You can work toward a meaningful life that does not involve a mate. You must make an effort to define your new life and create a "new normal" for yourself.

Exercise and Your Physical Health

Unfortunately, our current culture does not teach us that we can improve with age. But we can live longer and be healthier by including a healthy dose of exercise in our lifestyle. Exercise helps our bodies remain flexible and strong, and our heart muscle continues to be healthy. Decreased muscle mass and increased fat are not necessarily a natural part of aging, and we don't have to expect them as we grow older. Inactivity is their cause, accompanied by a mindset that we are expected to grow weaker as we age.

Exercise not only helps your heart stay strong and boosts your immune system, it also helps improve your mood. Even walking can help lower anxiety and stress.

Exercise plays an important role in maintaining both good physical and psychological health. Many doctors inform their patients of the benefits that exercise can give because it not only helps them become stronger physically, but also to helps alleviate their depression and anxiety.

While medication may help, exercise is a critical adjunct to achieving and maintaining a balanced emotional state. Exercise has positive effects on the brain, which occur through the release of endorphins, brain chemicals that have similar effects to those in highly addictive drugs such as morphine. Committing to exercising at least four times a week will make you feel better and you'll experience greater mind-body health.

The key to exercise is getting started. And it does take effort. We don't necessarily experience instant gratification either: there is an approximate 30-minute delay between when we begin exercising and when our bodies feel the effects of the endorphin release. Decide beforehand what type of exercise you want to do and where you want to do it. Choose comfortable clothes, and remember to have plenty of water on hand to stay adequately hydrated.

Creating a Support Network

If you have a loving family or supportive friends who include you for holidays, birthdays, or the occasional meal, you are very fortunate. By including you, they are helping to increase your confidence and self-esteem through their love and support.

Claire found that she needed time to "try on" the new persona that she was creating. She gained some self-confidence and was able to claim time to find herself; i.e., to discover the career that she wanted to pursue, to decide where she wanted to live, etc.

Claire and her daughter lived together and stayed busy with their respective school activities and responsibilities. Claire was not ready to devote time to another serious relationship. She did have a group of friends from church. Her "small group"—about eight or ten people that met usually at one another's homes—studied the Bible, prayed for one another, and shared one another's joys and sorrows. Their support helped Claire tremendously.

Claire knew she had to change some things to feel better and gain confidence in herself again. She took one step at a time every day and created this plan for "getting herself back":

Accept my feelings just as they are

Honestly experience my feelings

Participate in useful activities

Talk with trusted friends

Listen to radio, CDs, other inspirational media

Avoid indulgent behaviors

Exercise regularly

Examine my core beliefs

Realize that I am not alone

Family Adjustments

As parents approach divorce, their children experience dramatic adjustments. Their world is crumbling, too. In retrospect, Claire did not realize that her children suffered as much as they did. They were too young to have the vocabulary to describe the pain they felt.

When Claire and John's third child died, both she and her husband were understandably depressed. They were also exhausted, lonely, angry, and scared. They buried their grief in frequent travel.

Their daughter, Emily, was two years old then. Today she says that when her parents traveled, she thought they were never coming back. Their son Andrew, who was ten, pulled away emotionally and spent more time at his friends' homes.

After their parents' divorce, neither child was equipped to deal with the emotional fallout. Only as adults have they been able to express their feelings and gain closure to this painful period in their lives.

Case Study

Steve remembers his parents argued a lot when he was growing up. He remembers feeling the strain and distance between his mom and dad even when he was as young as three. His dad was a go-getter. His work was his passion. When the opportunity came to advance his career, he jumped at it, even though it meant relocating the family. In first grade, Steve had to make new friends, and get used to a new home and a new school.

Steve's dad was gone a lot of the time, learning the responsibilities of his new job. His mother was busy with getting the family settled. Then she got pregnant. There did not seem to be enough time for Steve in this equation, and he felt like a cog in the machine.

Steve recalls that living in his household was like living in the midst of a "cold war" with no playfulness, fun, or humor between his parents. In Steve's mind, his parents' relationship was more of a business arrangement than a loving marriage. He noticed that his friends' parents held hands, kissed, and even cuddled as they spoke to their children. Steve longed to have that kind of joy and love in his household.

Mealtimes—when everyone had to be together in the same room—seemed to him to be the worst time of day. There was no warm, pleasant conversation, only sarcasm and criticism. Steve was clever. He discovered that the sooner he finished his meal, the sooner he could go out and play, so that is just what he did. To this day, he has difficulties with digestion.

After his father left, Steve did not want to take on the role of the "man of the household" for his mother and little sister. He preferred to be independent, so he drove himself to school, and got a part-time job. He felt sad and lonely long into adulthood.

A divorcing parent's world is turned upside-down and he or she often experiences an emotional roller coaster of feelings such as anger, guilt, isolation, anxiety, depression, guilt, loss of control, fear, incompetence, and insecurity. It's important to remember that the children are hurting and scared as well. They are victims of the same situation that splintered the household and are also being forced to get used to the unfamiliar.

Some days you may be emotionally and physically drained, and feel as if you have failed your children and doubt your own worth. On those days, let your love for your children help you draw on your reserves of compassion and patience. Nurture your children by listening to them and giving them a lot of affection and reassurance. If they do not want to talk about the separation, help them express their feelings in other ways. A simple hug can convey that, together, you will survive this confusing time.

Each child reacts differently when one parent is suddenly no longer a part of the household. Some may regress to an earlier stage of development in times of stress. Their habits may change dramatically: they may gain or lose weight, or develop physical ailments. Some children may resort to violent behavior, or adopt questionable or illegal behaviors, such as smoking or drinking. Their self-esteem may suffer, and parents may witness a drop in grades or a declining ability to focus.

In *Talking to Children about Divorce: Ages and Stages*, authors Geraldine Bosch and Kim Bushaw provide a guide that helps parents identify what behavior a child might be experiencing because of the stress in the family due to impending separation and divorce. They categorized lists by the particular age of the child to help parents recognize and respond appropriately to their children's needs based on their developmental levels.

———⚬⚬⚬———

Common Response and Behaviors in Children of Divorce, Infant to Age Two

- Irritability or hyperactivity
- Difficulty sleeping
- Nightmares
- Crying
- Refusal to eat
- Upset digestive system
- Lack of response
- Clinginess
- Mimics the sad voices of others

How Parents Can Best Help

- Maintain consistent relationships with custodial parent, grandparents, and caregivers
- Visit regularly with your children without causing inconvenience to the children's regular schedule
- Extend generous amounts of affection, hugs, cuddling, and lap-time as needed

———⚬⚬⚬———

Common Response and Behaviors in Children of Divorce, Ages Three to Five

- Fear of abandonment and separation
- Fear of being alone
- Fear of losing parents' love

- Regression to bed wetting, thumb sucking, or baby talk
- Fantasies about parents getting back together
- When playing house, still including both Mom and Dad
- Changes in behavior
- Acting out aggressive behavior on dolls or toys
- Taking out anger on custodial parent
- Blaming themselves for a parent not being in the home anymore
- Having trouble remembering or learning
- Difficulty focusing on a task
- Appearing preoccupied
- Problems with sexual identity if same-sex parent is absent
- Symptoms of withdrawal

How Parents Can Best Help

- Keep reassuring your children that you love them
- Give your children assurance that they will see the other parent if this is so
- Keep telling children that the divorce is not their fault
- Tell your children how painful the divorce is for you, and how sorry you are that things can't be worked out
- Give your children specific information about where they will live and when visitation by the other parent will occur—a calendar might help
- Be as consistent as possible with day-to-day living
- Stop any hurtful actions, physical or verbal, toward yourself or others
- Listen to your children
- Substitute activities for aggression
- Keep parenting issues separate from post-marital tension
- Do not make negative comments about the other parent

- Keep your child involved with the same gender parent; if that person is not available, rely on relatives, child care providers, or mentoring programs for positive same-gender role models
- Never use your children to communicate with the other parent. If parents can't talk appropriately face-to-face or by phone, send letters or utilize a mediator
- Don't ask children to tell you about the other parent's dating behaviors
- Find other parents dealing with the same issues and talk with them

Common Response and Behaviors in Children of Divorce, Ages Six to Eight

- Panicky feelings that cause disorganized behavior
- Separation anxiety
- Frequent crying
- Nightmares about violence or disaster
- Attempting to take on the role of the protector, often destroying normal routines
- Expressing feelings of betrayal by parents
- Exhibiting more aggression and anger toward custodial parent
- May idealize the absent parent
- May experience issues with sex role identity if not in contact with their parent of the same sex
- Inability to let go and grieve
- Inability to focus and frequent distraction in learning or school work
- Belief that absent parent took an active and deliberate role in leaving

- Feelings of being unloved
- Making up stories about the parent who left
- Loneliness when living with one parent but not staying with the other
- Complaints of stomachaches or headaches
- Denial of discomfort or sadness
- Development of long-term unhealthy coping mechanisms, such as lying, stealing, or aggression
- Demanding more things (may even steal)
- Confusion and feelings of pressure to support one parent or the other
- May attempt to find another partner for a parent
- May exhibit a strong desire to try to get parents back together

How Parents Can Best Help

- Never suggest to children that they are "head of the house" now; often they take this literally
- Avoid trying to change your children's feelings; accept them as natural
- Both mother and father need to spend quality time with their child
- Include your child in some of your activities instead of being absent a lot of the time while working late, taking trips, going out with friends
- Don't talk negatively about the other parent
- Beware of quizzing your child after he/she has visited the other parent
- Have some fun times with your child to lighten up your situation
- Always reassure your children that you will be there for them and you love them

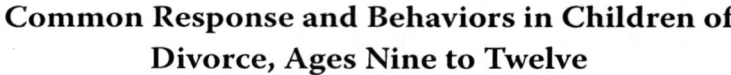

Common Response and Behaviors in Children of Divorce, Ages Nine to Twelve

- Displaying loyalty to both parents
- Highly expressive and frequently angry
- Using anger as a defense mechanism against hurt, depression, and shock
- Experiencing difficulty with puberty, especially if the same sex parent is not available
- Maintaining appearance of normalcy even when struggling
- Viewing parents as breaking the rules that he or she has been taught
- Trying to get back at the parent he or she thinks caused the divorce
- Feeling betrayed and lied to
- Manipulative behaviors such as "games" between parents
- Experiencing shame over what is happening to family
- Focusing on peers and their ideas of what is important
- Becoming confused about identity
- Experiencing headaches and stomachaches when parents argue
- Sometimes siding with one parent on issues

How Parents Can Best Help

- Don't choose your children as allies against the other parent
- Voice positive points about the other parent, especially since children at this age base their self-concept on their parents' perceptions of them
- Do not make statements about similarities to the

other parent
- Give children love and accept their feelings, even though it may be hard
- Keep your parenting style consistent and firm
- Help your children maintain a relationship with their same-sex parent, especially during puberty
- Involve your children in healthy activities
- Impress on children that they do belong and are important members of the family
- Schedule one-on-one time for children with each parent unless danger of abuse exists

Common Response and Behaviors in Children of Divorce, Ages Thirteen to Eighteen

- Exhibiting anger
- Turning against people or things because of parents' divorce
- Distancing parents
- Blaming parent he or she holds responsible for the divorce
- Becoming critical of parents and vowing to never make the same mistakes
- Taking the responsibility for younger children
- Having difficulty in choosing sides on issues regarding parents
- Appearing to be more mature than actual age
- Leaving, either physically or emotionally, to avoid family conflicts
- Becoming isolated, withdrawn, depressed, or even suicidal
- Becoming involved with drugs or alcohol, or exhibiting

promiscuous sexual behavior to escape
- Having difficulty seeing a parent dating again
- Having difficulty seeing parents expressing affection to new partners
- Getting involved in activities that are not age-appropriate, and trying to do too much
- Regressing to childish behaviors and becoming dependent again
- Lacking sense of where "home" is, especially after families have moved
- Doubting ability to follow through with a relationship when their parents failed
- Having a sense of relief that the constant conflict is over when the parents separate

How Parents Can Best Help

- Practice honesty with teens to avoid distrust
- Teach teens the power of negotiation
- Make no critical comments about the other parent
- Let teens have their own views about the other parent
- Have consistent rules and guidelines from both parents if possible
- Maintain stability and avoid big changes if you can
- Discuss teen's fears of being abandoned
- Encourage teens to see a counselor for support if necessary
- Do not view teens as the problem
- Do not overload teens with chores or tasks that were the other parent's duties
- Know who your teen's friends are, particularly at a new school
- Resist discussing your adult concerns such as financial

pressures, divorce proceedings, or the other parent's new relationship, which may cause the child to take on an adult role as they worry about the welfare of their parent
- Be aware that children benefit from contact with both parents in person or by phone

Parents are responsible for maintaining regular contact with the children. It is not in the best interest of a child for a parent to break his or her promises. A child can feel rejected, replaced, or just not important to the parent. When this scenario continually occurs, the child may develop behavioral problems.

Children need time to adjust to a one-parent home. They often continue to yearn for the other parent to return, particularly if they were close to that parent. Sometimes the parent who has custody has to move to a smaller residence, or even to a different state. This means that children have to leave their familiar surroundings and friends.

The following is as list of questions from The Parent/ Child Psychological Evaluation (www.divorcesource.com) to help you identify certain traits that show that your child may be having significant problems:

1. Is your child having academic problems?
2. Are there sudden changes in weight, either loss/gain?
3. Is your child rebelling against normal activities or routine?
4. Does your child refuse to eat or have eating problems?
5. Does your child constantly eat to help himself/herself feel better?
6. Does your child have problems with sleeping?

7. Does your child display secretive behavior, such as closing the bedroom door?

8. Does your child complain excessively about headaches or stomachaches?

9. Does your child cry a lot or seem overly emotional?

10. Is your child experiencing dramatic mood swings?

11. Does your child deny that any problems exist?

12. Does your child revert to earlier stages of development?

13. Does your child always resist visiting the other parent?

14. Does your child resist authority both by parents and teachers?

15. Are there sudden changes in your child's appearance?

Part III

Moving On

"When a door to happiness
closes, another opens;
but often we look so long
at the closed door
that we do not see the one
which has opened for us."

Lao-tsu

Gaining Momentum

When a couple separates, they disconnect from one another. If the decision was made by one and not the other, the partner that is left to pick up the pieces may have a hard time adjusting to living life on his or her own.

Disconnecting from the Past

Depending on how close you were to your spouse, you may feel as if part of you is gone. You may have depended on your spouse for love, security, and companionship. The unfamiliar circumstances in which you find yourself may feel scary.

Disconnecting from your past and beginning a new lifestyle is a process. It may require that you develop a new self-image and redefine who you are without your spouse.

Learning to Cope with the Changes

Claire didn't want her life to change, but it did. Her husband no longer came home at night. She did not know how much money she had to spend or where she would live. Claire would awake every morning and wonder what that day would bring. She felt so alone. All the decisions were up to her. She had to begin taking responsibility because there was no one else on whom she could depend.

The speed with which you rebuild your life depends on the timing and circumstances of the breakup of the relationship and how much time and energy you have had to invest in your grief. Comparing how you are grieving with others is not healthy. Some people can get started right away whereas others may take one to two years or longer after the relationship has ended.

If you find that you are having a hard time moving forward in your life and feel that you are "stuck," you may need professional counseling.

Here are some signs to look for:

- You cannot carry out simple tasks at work or home
- You begin to develop risky behaviors such as drinking too much
- You have obsessive thoughts about harming yourself or others
- You experience significant weight gain or weight loss
- You feel that you are stuck in your pain and cannot go on living
- You need help in identifying a new direction to go in your life

If any of these symptoms emerge, look for a licensed counselor or psychologist. You may have a friend who knows a good therapist. If you have medical insurance call the number listed on your member card. Or, go to the website of your insurance company, where you will find mental health practitioners listed.

Case Study

Alice didn't know what was wrong with her husband George. He seemed irritable all the time. When things went wrong, George always blamed Alice.

They didn't communicate. George made impulsive decisions without consulting her, including buying a new car. Alice could feel that they were growing apart. Still she continued cooking, cleaning, and taking care of whatever he requested. And her husband continued to complain and criticize. In truth, she felt more like his mother than his wife.

One Saturday night, George's temper erupted. He accused Alice of being a horrible wife and said he was leaving. He packed some things and checked into a local hotel. The next day he called Alice to say he'd been thinking about how boring their marriage was and that he wanted a divorce.

Alice never believed that George would ever leave her. She had grown up with a father and mother who argued constantly, so she thought that was what a marriage was. Her husband had always belittled her, but, too afraid of being alone, she let him treat her with disrespect. She had tolerated his behavior for years. This was life as she knew it. Now life would be different. Alice wondered if she could let go of her past and focus on her future. She wasn't used to making decisions that had outcomes that she desired. Alice needed to regain her confidence and stop replaying old tapes in her head—George's voice saying that she was no good, she was boring, she was an idiot. Alice needed to disconnect.

Making Adjustments

It may take months to adjust to your new life as a single person. You must gather all your courage and determination in order to embrace the many changes unfolding in your life.

A strong faith can help you get through the worst circumstances. Claire discovered this for herself during the divorce process. She prayed a lot. When she felt no one else understood, Claire talked to God. Going to church had been important to her family when she was young and it became even more important to her after she was separated from her husband. Claire had nowhere else to turn, and her belief became stronger. As she sat in the church service, she felt God's presence and comfort.

Claire and her children belonged to a church in Virginia at the time of her separation from her husband. Claire went to church even after her husband left. Though she felt embarrassed at first, the congregation was very supportive.

Your old life may have revolved around couples. When you divorce, your interests and needs change. It's no longer the familiar "us," but just "me." You need to find people in the community who will help you. Surround yourself with people who are trustworthy and dependable. With determination, you can adapt to your new lifestyle.

If your husband always took care of the car problems, then you'll need to find a dependable mechanic who is willing to help you in a crisis. Ask him or her to teach you how to check the oil, put air in the tires, and top off the fluids. The American Automobile Association (AAA) is a helpful service for single women to consider. For a reasonable fee, they are a phone call away should anything happen to your car.

Claire's mechanic knew that she was a single mom and he was a great help when her battery died one morning as she was leaving for work. He called a tow truck, which took Claire and her car to the service station. A new battery was installed and Claire was on her way to work without losing much time at all.

Responsibilities around the house came to include mowing the grass, which was a new skill for Claire. She also had to maintain the lawn mower, change the oil, and sharpen the blades. A screen blew off an attic window and she had no idea how to get it back in place. Claire learned.

If you have children, one of the problems that may immediately arise is childcare. You and your spouse may have shared that responsibility. Maintaining a friendly relationship with your former spouse will prove to be beneficial. Having discussions with your spouse about the children's activities and carpooling responsibilities makes everyone's life easier, especially your children's.

If you are relocating, you also must find medical doctors, dentists, and, if you have pets, veterinarians.

Case Study

After Jan and Don had a child, Don was the more active, responsible parent. Don enjoyed spending time with their four-year-old son, Josh, and when they were together, Don had as much fun as his son. Jan had a career with a local bank and often had to work well into the night. Don was always there to feed Josh his dinner, read him a story, and put him to bed.

When Jan demanded a divorce, Don was sad that he would not see his son as much. Their custody agreement was that they would share equal custody, but Don had always been the major caregiver, so "equal" time actually meant less time for him. Still working late hours, Jan often had to hire sitters to care for Josh in the evenings. Wanting to see Josh as much as he could, Don volunteered to pick up Josh from daycare and bring him home with him so he could sleep over at his house when Jan worked late. Jan was very agreeable with this arrangement, and Josh was the biggest winner.

It is hard to adjust to the many "firsts" that come the first year of the break-up of a relationship. Among the painful "first" events without your spouse are your wedding anniversary and birthday, Christmas, Super Bowl party, backyard barbeque, family vacation, and graduation of a child from school or college. You may dread these special occasions because they emphasize your loss. However, there is no way to avoid them.

One of Claire's "firsts" was Thanksgiving. She and her children were alone, but still she cooked a traditional Thanksgiving dinner. An awkward silence pervaded the room, whereas in years past it was a festive occasion and included some of their relatives.

The next year they went to Claire's mother's home where they were received with warmth and caring. They left their memories of the past behind them. Although they still thought of happier times, that Thanksgiving was much more gratifying.

Shifting to New Behaviors and Beliefs

When you are at a low point in your life, it may be difficult to build your confidence. Some questions may arise like, "What do I need?" and, "What do I have to offer?" One way of moving on is to let go of your old ways and stop blaming yourself or your former spouse. It is time to create a new self.

Evaluating Your Strengths

Make a list of things that you like about yourself. For instance, you always arrive for an appointment on time, or you are an organized person. Be proud of yourself for possessing those particular attributes.

After her divorce, Claire found it difficult at first to identify any personal strengths. She had little self-esteem or confidence, and it took her several years to create a "new normal."

Her life as a congressional wife was very different from her new life as a single mom. She had to change her entire concept of who she was, and what she was capable of doing. In her former life, she had the luxury of an interior designer. In her new life, she chose the color and fabric for the drapes. She decided on the placement of furniture in each room. Before the separation, she had a housekeeper who cooked most of the family's meals. Now she was forced to be mindful of food prices and tried to be as thrifty as possible.

Claire began to rely on and trust her judgment instead of looking to others for advice or help. Eventually, she realized that she had the power to make wise choices and the determination needed to see them to completion.

Learning from your past experiences is an important part of creating a new reality. So, you'll need to identify and evaluate any negative patterns that you had in your former relationship.

Was your relationship balanced? Or, were you a "giver" and your spouse a "taker?" Did you depend on him or her too much and forfeit decision-making power? How responsible were you in the marriage? By learning how to recognize imbalances, you are more likely to establish more balanced relationships in the future.

If your thoughts about yourself are so negative that you can't identify any positive traits, seek professional help with a licensed therapist. Therapists are trained to listen and support you in your goals and they can show you how to get started. They can teach you what healthy love relationships are.

There are support groups for singles, such as Parents Without Partners and Divorce Lifeline. You may find supportive friends there because you will have common interests.

Dealing with Stress

Claire took some stress inventories that confirmed how stressed she felt because sometimes she felt as if she was "going crazy." She began educating herself about stress and its devastating effects. Many people think stress is another way of saying tension or pressure. However, stress is a demand made on the capacity of the mind to respond and adapt to change. If you have the capacity to handle stress, you respond well. If you don't have the capacity to respond to stress, you will let it overpower you.

Stress can be both good and bad. If you have the capacity to deal with the demand and enjoy the stimulation involved, then stress is welcome and helpful. Examples are: going on vacation or moving to another home. Claire's stress was caused by more chronic problems, such as trying to earn a master's degree while working, worrying about finances, and feeling guilty about not giving her daughter enough of her time.

Events are not so much the cause of your stress as your reactions to them. Understanding what stresses you and how it affects you can help you make positive changes to reduce these stressors and live a healthier life.

Noted psychiatrists Thomas Holmes and Richard Rahe developed a scale in 1967 that supports the links between stress and illness. This scale is included in Appendix A on page 139.

Physiological Changes During Stress

Many physiological changes in the body are due to stress. As the body tries to deal with the stressor and yet keep the body in balance, the body makes certain adjustments to help compensate. The body secretes stress hormones to tackle the situation. This response is known as the "fight or flight" response.

When the body encounters a stressful condition, the "fight or flight" response is activated. First the hypothalmus is alerted. This part of the brain controls and secretes different hormones into the body. It starts by secreting a hormone called Adenocorticotrophic-releasing hormone (ARH). Secretion of the ARH stimulates the pituitary gland, situated below the hypothalamus, to secrete Adenocortico-trophic hormone (ACTH). The ACTH then stimulates the adrenal glands located on top of the kidneys to secrete the stress hormones adrenaline and cortisol. Both of these hormones are responsible for the physiological effects of stress through the "fight or flight" response by making adjustments in the body.

Every time you encounter stress, your body gets ready physiologically to help you. Your heart beats faster and your blood pressure instantly rises as your body goes into "fight or flight" mode. Other signs and symptoms are:

- tense muscles
- clenched jaw
- grinding teeth during sleep
- backaches
- chest pain
- heart palpitations
- cold, clammy skin
- hot flashes
- breathlessness
- dry mouth
- stomachache
- ulcers
- diarrhea
- headaches
- loss of energy

- forgetfulness
- sleeplessness
- lack of sexual drive
- loss of appetite
- anxiety
- depression
- inability to manage anger

Short-Term Stress

With short-term stress, once the stressor is gone, the symptoms of stress disappear. Short-term stress causes the following physiological changes in the body:

- Blood supply diverts from less vital organs to more vital organs
- The heart rate increases for quicker blood supply
- Blood pressure increases for greater blood supply
- Increased respiratory rate increases oxygen supply from the atmosphere
- Breakdown of glycogen in the liver and muscle for more glucose

Long-Term Stress

When the stress is persistent and chronic and there appears to be no solution to the problem(s) causing the stress, symptoms for these stressors are more severe:

- migraine headaches
- mood swings
- alcohol or drug abuse
- memory deficits

- heart attack
- stroke
- weight loss
- irritable bowel disease
- Crohn's disease
- decreased sexual drive
- inability to sleep

Effects of Stress on Organs and Systems of the Body

The brain, cardiovascular system, respiratory system, non-vital organs, and immune system are all affected by stress.

The limbic system, located in the temporal lobe of the brain, controls emotions and is affected by the stress hormones. Anxiety, mood swings, and depression are a result of the stress hormones on the limbic system.

The hormone adrenaline acts on the receptor sites of the heart. The receptors are chemical substances present in the wall of the heart, which, combined with adrenaline, result in the stimulation of the heart, causing an increase in rate and force of contraction of the heart muscle. The result is increased cardiac output. Adrenaline also acts on receptor sites in the walls of the blood vessels increasing blood pressure. Therefore, blood is delivered more effectively to various tissues in the body.

Stress hormones act on the lungs, causing increased respiratory rate. More oxygen enters the lungs and more blood is taken to various tissues.

The blood supply to the less vital organs—such as the spleen, gastrointestinal tract, and skin—is decreased so that the more vital organs like the brain and heart will receive more blood supply. The gastrointestinal tract is deprived of blood supply resulting in poor digestion. The skin becomes cold and clammy.

The immune system experiences increased levels of cortisol, a steroid. Cortisol suppresses the immune system resulting in increased vulnerability to infections. With prolonged stress, illness is likely to occur more frequently.

Balancing Stress in Your Life

Balance in your life is key. It is not healthy to have too much stress or even too little stress. It is important to use the energy we get from stress to meet life's challenges and reach our goals.

In Appendix B (page 142), you'll find a stress test that will help you to evaluate your stress in different categories of your life. Use it as an educational tool to identify areas of your life in which you are experiencing more stress. The test is divided into several categories: emotional, physical, social, spiritual, and work. The more checks that you put in each category, the higher your stress level.

Four characteristics that determine your response to stress are: heredity, lifestyle, personality, and support system.

Heredity

Examine your family tree to find out if your parents, grandparents, aunts and uncles, or brothers and sisters had any health conditions that might have been caused by stress.

Some such illnesses might be heart attack or stroke. Some family members might have abused drugs or alcohol.

They might have suffered from anxiety, depression, or post-traumatic stress disorder (PTSD). Becoming familiar with your family health history can help you realize how you can deal with your stress in a healthy way.

Lifestyle

Lifestyle is another characteristic that will determine your stress response. Having an exercise routine, eating a healthy diet, and learning how to relax will help you manage daily stressors.

Change requires a flexible lifestyle.

Personality

There are personality traits that a person prone to stress will exhibit. Turn to Appendix C (page 146) to identify the personality traits of a stress-prone individual. You will find a rating scale so you can assess how often you experience those traits yourself. Then ask yourself if there are any traits that you want to change.

If you would like to identify your personality type, turn to Appendix D (page 148). You will find the Jung Typology Test, which is based on the Jung-Myers-Briggs personality approach. It provides you with knowledge about your strengths and preferences, as well as a description of your personality type.

Ten Traits of a Flexible Person

I embrace change. Relish change and have confidence in your ability to deal with it. Your confidence is a result of acknowledging previous successes.

I initiate change in my life. Try new foods, different magazines, different clothes, new ways of doing things. Create new interests and new traditions.

I encourage initiative. New projects are undertaken without assurances of success. Be willing to risk not seeing yourself as a failure, but giving yourself credit for trying.

I like variety in my activities at work and in my personal life. Let go of responsibilities and tasks and either replace them or take on different ones. Discard ideas or items that are no longer useful. Give away clothing, books, or other items you no longer need.

I take time to make decisions. Put ideas on hold for a while.

I don't have to be perfect. Recognize mistakes and have a sense of humor about them.

I have some fun in life. Build amusing elements into your work life and personal life.

I encourage different thinking and change styles. Surround yourself with a variety of friends, professional colleagues, and relatives—young and old, educated or ignorant—and intently listen to their opinions.

I accept that there will always be change in my life. Know that disequilibrium is an ever-changing constant.

I learn more from the future than from the past. Look ahead and discover what you should be doing currently.

Support System

A good support system is important in handling stress. Cultivate relationships that offer guidance, feedback, material assistance, and emotional encouragement to cope with the unexpected demands of life. Identify people in your life who help you through crises and with whom feelings can be shared without fear and condemnation. Associate with groups of people who can be relied upon to always be a friend to you and even provide help and resources if you need it. Associate with friends who share your standards and values.

Turn to Appendix D (page 148) to evaluate the qualities of people that you need in your social support system. Do the individuals you now know have the qualities you need and would be helpful to you at this time in your life?

Relaxation Techniques to Reduce Stress

It is important to learn how to relax when combating stress. The following are several stress-reducing activities:

- aerobic exercise
- visualization
- any concentrated task, such as sculpting, knitting, painting, etc.
- muscle-relaxation methods
- meditation
- laughter

Exercise Reduces Stress

Exercise relaxes the mind and body, burns fat, improves cardiovascular health, helps you breathe in more oxygen, lowers blood pressure, and reduces the likelihood of disease. Regular exercise helps us manage the "fight or flight" response and helps the body return to a balanced state more quickly. It is one of the best ways to manage stress.

Many women have had negative experiences with exercise. Bad school memories or just negative cultural influences tend to emphasize athletic skills rather than fitness. Author John Douillard reports that more than 50 percent of women experience their first major failure while participating in organized physical activities such as gym class.

Consequently, many girls feel that they are not good in sports. They may consider themselves "physical losers" all their lives.

Your past history may prevent you from forming a positive association with exercise. To help you develop a healthy attitude about exercise, examine what caused your negative feelings about it. List your early experiences with physical activity and sports. Ask yourself what felt good and what you liked. Explore your core beliefs about exercise and sports. Then list all the benefits that you know that come from exercise. This may get you started in a good exercise program.

According to Patty Andrews, ACTP, (Adobe Certified Training Provider), there are many reasons why exercise is important in our lives. First, after exercising, your alertness is increased. Tension in your body is reduced and your body moves more easily. Exercise helps our bodies become fit and therefore gives us more confidence in our social skills and gives us the discipline to perform tasks/activities we would be less likely to pursue. Intuition is also enhanced because repetitive movement increases the alpha waves in the brain. The alpha state is associated with enhanced intuition.

The benefits of regular, moderate exercise include:

- decreased risk of heart disease
- healthier immune system
- lower overall cancer rate
- decreased risk of breast cancer
- increased longevity
- less depression and anxiety
- relaxation, more assertiveness, spontaneity, and enthusiasm
- stronger bones
- restful sleep
- higher self-esteem

- more energy
- fewer premenstrual syndrome (PMS) symptoms
- improved weight control

The four types of exercise that are important for good health are: aerobic exercise, strength training, stretching, and breathing.

Aerobic Exercise

Aerobic exercise includes; walking, running, swimming, and bicycling. Aerobic exercise keeps your heart and lungs in good condition and burns excess fat. Aerobic exercise results in increased energy level which can help you feel more social and outgoing. You may develop a better self-image of your body, which increases your confidence, and improves your self-esteem and self-worth.

To reap the benefit of aerobic exercise, you must reach 60 to 80 percent of your target heart rate for at least 20 minutes, three to five times a week. To calculate your target heart rate, refer to Appendix E (page 149).

Strength Training

If you don't exercise, you lose about a half pound of muscle per year. Muscle loss results in fat gain. Therefore, as you age, you can gain 1.5 pounds of fat per year.

Weight-bearing exercises and strength training help increase muscle mass and keep bones strong. You will find that with strength training, the more you lift, the easier everything gets. Working opposing groups of muscles, such as triceps and biceps, or quadriceps and hamstrings, helps maintain the ability to balance, a function that diminishes with age. Yoga and Pilates are good ways to strengthen muscles in the hips, stomach, and back.

Stretching

Stretching is important before, and especially after, exercise. Stretching helps prevent injury and allows for greater freedom of movement. It increases the blood flow to the muscles and helps remove lactic acid, which prevents soreness after you exercise. Good times to stretch are also when you are sitting at your desk and feel your muscles tighten or when you feel your shoulders rising up under your ears.

Breathing

Breathing is one of the most important parts of any exercise routine. The correct way to breathe is through your nose. Mouth breathing is a sign of stress. Gulping air through your mouth results in a higher heart rate and breath rate. Nose breathing is associated with parasympathetic and sympathetic nervous system balance.

Take a moment and compare the two different methods of breathing: mouth breathing versus nose breathing. First, take three full, deep breaths through your mouth. Next take three full, deep breaths through your nose. Be aware of how your breath goes all the way to the lower lobes of your lungs when you breathe through your nose.

If you breathe through your nose when you exercise, your lungs will work more efficiently and you will be able to achieve higher levels of fitness without as much effort.

If you have trouble getting started with exercise, you

may want to consider working with a personal trainer. Your trainer should review your medical history and conduct an activity profile, which will help define your fitness goals. An exercise plan should include strength training, cardiovascular flexibility, and core exercises.

A good trainer will encourage you to be committed and be willing to work hard both safely and effectively. Ask if your personal trainer has any experience with nutrition, as that is an important component of healthy living.

If you are exercising to reduce body fat, Andrews recommends eating five times a day (three main meals and two snacks), which is better for the metabolism. She suggests eating foods that are high in fiber and low in fat, sodium, and sugar. She advocates avoiding processed foods and suggests that her clients gravitate toward foods in their natural nutritional state. This will help sustain energy throughout the day. She also encourages her clients to drink lots of water because dehydration can make you feel tired and sluggish.

Use the HALT (hungry, angry, lonely, tired) method to check in with yourself to see what might be causing a lack of energy. When you identify a symptom you can do something about it. For example, hunger might indicate low blood sugar.

Recall anything that may have happened to you in the past few days that causes you to feel angry. Your family may live too far away to visit often, causing you to feel lonely. Or, you have too much to get accomplished in your daily schedule and feel exhausted. If any one of these symptoms sounds familiar, think about what you can do to resolve the situation.

By controlling your stress through exercise and the other methods mentioned, you're ready to focus on your future.

Dreaming to Discover Your Passion

Ask yourself who you are at this time in your life and where you want to go. Change that lasts isn't instant or easy. It takes time and you may have some rough spots before you reach your goal.

Shifting around your old beliefs and behaviors takes time. The secret is to keep working at it until the new positive behavior becomes a habit. You are creating a life that reflects your new values.

As Claire confronted how she wanted to change her life, she realized change isn't for sissies. Shifting how you see your life is a painful, scary process. You stay stuck unless you shift your thought process. Often it takes extreme discomfort to force you to make change.

Going Back to School

One of the major changes Claire made was choosing a career path, one which required that she return to school. She found that going to school as an adult with children while holding down a job was an entirely different experience than when she attended college in her early twenties. At that time, she just got a general degree with a focus on teaching. She didn't work and could live anywhere she wanted. She wasn't married and she didn't have children.

Claire considered how much time it would take weekly for her to go to class and also do her homework, and she found that she could make the time. She chose to go to a local university. She enrolled in their counseling program and began working towards her master's degree.

Claire was somewhat intimidated by being in school again. She was older than most of the students. Claire hadn't written a paper or taken a test in years, and she was afraid that she wouldn't succeed. She didn't have the luxury of living in a dorm or an apartment near campus, so she couldn't walk to the library anytime she wanted. She worked during the day, and then sped to her class, which was forty-five minutes away. After class, she returned home to give her daughter supper and help her finish her homework.

Claire had always enjoyed learning new things and found it invigorating to be in the classroom environment. She could appreciate the value of what she was learning because she realized that she'd be using it with clients soon. Being an adult student revealed new opportunities. Not only was she learning new material, but she met fellow adults.

Going back to school opened a new door in her life because that is how she found her new career and herself. Here is a checklist to help you decide if you really want to go back to school:

- How will this degree help make your life better?
- What type of jobs will be available to you?
- Do you have passion for the job that you seek?
- How much time will it take to attend class and complete homework?
- Can you fit school into your current schedule?
- Can you afford to go back to school?

- How far is the school from your home?
- When can you expect to graduate?
- Do you have the ability to focus and the energy to participate?

Starting a Business

If going back to school isn't for you, you may want to consider going into business for yourself. The following are some steps in starting your own business:

- Consider your income and if you have enough money
- Assess how much energy and time you have each day to spend on your work
- Realistically determine whether or not you have sufficient contacts to be successful
- Your needs may vary according to the type of business you have, but find a place that suits your proposed business
- Find out what kind of maintenance is needed or provided for your proposed workspace
- Make sure the office has the amenities you need, such as a bathroom or kitchen space if you need it
- Select an office in which there are no safety concerns
- Research the insurance requirements for your business
- Determine how you will advertise your business
- If you have children, determine childcare needs, including a back-up plan for emergencies
- Determine how much money you can make the first six months, first year, two years, etc.
- Research health benefits and coverage for self-employed business owners

- Find a trustworthy friend who is familiar with your
  work with whom you can share joys and concerns

As a beginning counselor, Claire worked with a mental health group so she could gain experience. However after several years she decided to work alone as a counseling professional. She had developed a network of professional colleagues who would refer their clients to her and eventually she had a large enough clientele to start her own business.

After much searching, Claire did find a ten-story building where she could afford to rent an office on the fourth floor. The property managers were willing to paint the walls and provide new carpet. Restrooms were nearby and available on the same floor as her office. The building had several elevators, was located on a bus line, had a well lit parking lot, and was accessible for handicapped people. So Claire hung out her shingle and began offering counseling services.

It is important to have a detailed plan of what your company would look like, then stick to your plan. Set goals for your first year and then assess if you met them. Revise your plan as needed. You might find it helpful to hire a coach or specialist to help you create a business plan.

Discovering, Reclaiming or Reaffirming Your Spirituality

We are all spiritual beings. Our spirituality is our awareness of our connection to a higher power and the oneness of all. Our fundamental beliefs and values determine basically who we are and how we view the world. Our thought patterns influence our motives for making choices and determine the amount of confidence we have to make things happen for us.

If you have no confidence in yourself and don't believe that you can succeed, it will affect the way other people view you. If your belief is that you don't have to work hard at your job, but think that life owes you something, the result is you will probably not keep that job very long.

The thoughts that we have are at the very center of our belief about the world. Some of these thought patterns that filter our beliefs are optimism vs. pessimism. Having confidence that we can change our old beliefs about ourselves helps us reach our goals through our new thought patterns.

Exciting new research is being done by authors Gregg Braden, Bruce Lipton, and Sharon Begley about how the mind can be transformed through training. This research has shown that the way people think changes their brains.

When we willfully think certain thoughts in certain ways, we can restore mental health. People with depression have learned how to think differently about thoughts that might lead them to relapse. They have learned that by thinking certain thoughts, they can increase activity in one area of the brain and decrease it in another.

Immediately following her divorce, Claire was very hard on herself and pessimistic about what her quality of life would be. She started reading self-help books on how people survive divorce. Claire asked others how they had learned to cope with their lives, and she was referred to a counselor who both understood and supported her.

After several months, Claire's beliefs about herself and her life started changing. She began believing that she had the power to change her circumstances and to live a satisfying life. And because she believed she could, Claire did.

Claire truly thought that she could live a fulfilling life with good friends and a career that she enjoyed. As she went about her day, her attitude began to reflect that. She looked forward to each day with hope and gratitude and her life began changing.

If you continue to wallow in guilt and anger, then you will find that other dissatisfied people come into your life, such as family members, fellow co-workers or friends who are down on life. All of you are miserable together. This is the law of attraction.

To help get you moving from pessimism to optimism, surround yourself with individuals who see their glass half full (not half empty) and who will support you in moving on in your life.

When author Gina Ogden conducted a study on divorce and women's spirituality, she found that more than 80 percent of the women sought counseling, which facilitated healing, indicating that tapping spiritual strength was an important factor in post-divorce.

Case Study

Peggy and her mother had been very close. Her mother was so happy when Peggy told her she was marrying Mike. Not only was Mike handsome, he also made a lot of money. Peggy's mother and Mike became good friends.

Mike and Peggy had been married a year when Mike began voicing dissatisfaction with everything Peggy did. Nothing Peggy did suited her husband. He would become angry when she went out with her girlfriends. He felt that she should spend all her time on their home and yard and run errands for him, such as picking up his dry cleaning.

One night, Mike's anger grew into rage over a trivial incident, and he hit Peggy with his fist. Peggy decided she had had enough, and she left her husband.

When Peggy tried to get advice from her mother, her mother always took Mike's side. Her mother couldn't believe that this was the same man who talked with her in such a friendly, respectful way. Although she loved her mother, Peggy had to find someone else to listen to her problems.

It is up to you to take responsibility for making better choices. Learn from your past mistakes. As you begin to move forward in your life, focus on what is going right, not what is wrong. If negative thoughts absorb us, they can become a self-fulfilling prophecy. Thoughts are very powerful. Begin by having the expectation that good things are going to happen. This is the law of attraction. Saturate your mind with that belief.

Begin your day by breathing in and out slowly. Breathe in to a count of four and blow out through your mouth to a count of six. Ask your breath to take you to what you want.

Create an idea in your mind of what you would like your future to be and imagine it. Remember that anything is possible. Think about what you would like your future relationships to be like and what kind of job you would like to have. Imagine the kind of house you would like to live in and what hobbies you would enjoy. Envision what you would like for your life to look like and believe that you can have it.

How does one begin a journey of self-awareness?

Breath awareness and conscious breathing are useful tools to those seeking personal growth. Although individuals today acknowledge that conscious breathing is a component of good health, optimum performance, and ultimate potential, many have not developed conscious breathing skills. Here's how you can do it.

When your mind is quiet, an inner process occurs, or a "knowing," in which you feel more focused and find clearer answers that you could not discover in your daily hustle and bustle. The following are some characteristics of the inner process, or getting in touch with our intuition:

- Achieves a slower pace or rhythm
- Explores logic of wholes and relationships revealed in images, metaphors, feelings, and movements or gestures
- Is inclusive of many perceptions of experience
- Moves and shifts in its own time
- Comes freely and does not respond to force or power

You will gain peace and balance as well as answers to your questions about life when you learn how to focus your mind. Answers will come to you with greater ease.

If you want to work on self-improvement, you can explore the potential and power of breathing with a counselor, coach, or therapist. Even athletes can benefit by learning about the power of the breath. By controlling and directing your breath, you can learn to regulate your physiological, emotional, psychological, and spiritual states.

Jungian analyst Leah Berne teaches breathwork to help her clients relax so that they can explore new possibilities in their experience. Breathing is a natural, unceasing function of life. It connects an individual to both inner and outer worlds. It can serve as a guide to lead our body and our mind into a greater expansion of both inner and outer spaces.

One thought—such as, "I must hurry to catch the bus"—can change your breathing pattern. You will sense a tightness and shallow breathing as you fear you might be late. Conversely, when thinking of something pleasant in your life, your breathing is more relaxed and expansive. Your breathing pattern is influenced by your emotions, including anytime you become upset or agitated.

There are many upsetting situations every day which cause our breath to shrink. A boss may criticize the way an employee does a job or a teacher might get angry at a child for not following directions. Even the ambitious, angry boss who is climbing the political ladder at work and uses her breath only to carry out her driving ambitions will at some point become breathless and unable to achieve her goals anymore.

See Appendix G (on page 153) for a two-minute breathing exercise aimed at making you calmer and more focused and perhaps afford you more insight regarding your problems.

When our bodies need fluids, we become thirsty and we have a desire to drink. When we quench our thirst, our bodies respond with gratitude and joy. Doesn't a cool glass of water taste wonderful when the weather is hot? Just like our bodies crave water, we all desire meaning in our lives. The more we feel our lives are going in the right direction, the more joy we feel.

So how do we find what gives us that profound joy and avoid whatever causes us to experience pain?

The universe offers us clues every step of the way.

Some ways to recognize when we are on track is when we feel inspired or when you become passionate or deeply enthusiastic about something. We are on track when we find what gives us a sense of enjoyment.

All of us have only so much time each day. So begin every day by surrounding yourself with people and situations that bring you joy.

The great spiritual master, Rumi, wrote that our bodies are like a guest house that invites new guests in every day. We must welcome all guests—regardless of the positive or negative baggage they carry—because each has been sent to us to guide us through life.

As Claire began to look deeper into her life and practice breathwork, she began to realize that her broken marriage was not just her husband's fault. She needed to change, too. Claire had emotional baggage that she needed to address and discard. Taking responsibility for behavior and thought processes that need to change requires strength and courage. Claire asked for divine help to give her courage and to help her heal the emotional issues buried deep inside of her. The new Claire slowly began to emerge.

Here are some ways you may explore to achieve your own inner peace:

- Use visual imagery to picture in your mind a peaceful scene, such as ripples of the ocean on a starry night that dance like diamonds
- Say some peaceful words slowly: serenity, calm, quiet, tranquility
- Find some favorite lines of poetry to read silently or aloud
- Choose peaceful words to express your thoughts and feelings
- Practice the habit of silence for at least one or two minutes every day—or start with fifteen seconds and be accepting of that
- Turn off cell phones, PDAs, beepers, or other gadgets that create noise

- Form pictures in your mind of uplifting experiences from your past or in your life now
- Avoid punishing yourself for anything you have done; practice forgiveness instead

Dr. Jon Kabat-Zinn, an expert on stress reduction, teaches that it is all in the attitude with which we live each day. The following are some spiritual principles that can help you get to know yourself on a deeper, spiritual level.

Spiritual Principles to Live by Each Day

- Assume a nonjudgmental attitude as you go about your day
- Develop patience, accepting that things will unfold in their own time
- Develop an attitude of seeing things as if for the first time, free of dredging up negative past experiences
- Trust in yourself and your feelings
- Learn to let go of excess "baggage" that you may be carrying around
- Let go of anger
- Release any worry
- Work diligently
- Have a grateful spirit
- Be kind to others

Appendix H (on page 154) outlines an exercise to help quiet your spirit so that you can discover answers within yourself.

Pursuing and Enjoying
Healthy Relationships

Just because we are attracted to someone doesn't mean that the attraction will lead to a healthy relationship.

When Claire met her husband, they were both in college. After graduation, they dated for a year or so. Claire thought that in that length of time they had gotten to know one another well. They were both 22 years old when they married. They failed, however, to discuss basic issues in their relationship, such as trust, loyalty, responsibility, children, finances, work issues, and their individual needs. Their families were compatible, but they did not seriously discuss their core beliefs and values about life. Claire and John just assumed that they agreed on everything.

There are eight "must have" characteristics of a satisfying, healthy love relationship: mutual respect, trust, honesty, responsibility, good communication, unselfishness, separate identities, and sexual compatibility.

Mutual Respect

A relationship that has mutual respect is one in which both people are aware of one another's boundaries and do not abuse them. Neither tells the other what to do. This is hard for some people (particularly controlling individuals). Although you and your partner may think differently about an issue, you can learn to discuss the problem and compromise.

Case Study

Adam wanted Jane to go with him every Saturday night when he visited his family. After all he was his parent's favorite son and it was always great to listen to them brag about his accomplishments! They'd eat dinner together and later sit around and talk. Adam's mom disagreed with Jane's child-rearing tactics, and also had issues with the fact that her daughter-in-law worked. Jane became very defensive, and tension built between mother-in-law and daughter-in-law. Predictably, when they got together, an argument ensued. Jane's feelings were hurt when no one came to her defense. Finally, because there was never respect for her feelings, Jane refused to visit her husband's parents. Adam didn't understand, and this became a major problem in their marriage.

When Jane threatened to leave him, Adam realized that he had to do something. He listened to Jane as she explained how emotionally distraught and angry she felt. Adam and Jane agreed to compromise. Jane would not go with Adam every time he went to visit his parents. Adam informed his parents that he would drop by to see them every other weekend, but that he and Jane wanted to spend some Saturday nights together doing things that they enjoyed. Adam developed respect for his wife's feelings and their marriage survived.

Trust

The foundation of any good relationship is trust. If you can't trust your spouse and are constantly worried about where he/she is or what he/she is doing, life becomes frustrating and exhausting. A lack of trust erodes your confidence. A healthy relationship is impossible without trust.

It is also important to trust yourself and believe in your own basic wisdom. Be your own person and learn to trust your intuition. Often one partner does not want to believe that the other partner is being untruthful or unfaithful. Too many individuals remain in a relationship far too long because they believe that "it could ever happen to me!"

In a committed relationship, you trust your partner to be loyal to you.

Trust can also be betrayed by one member of the relationship by gossiping about the other to friends or buddies. Examples of when this might happen include when friends get together to watch a ballgame or go shopping. Never divulge negative qualities about your partner to your children. Don't discuss your marital issues with anyone other than a trusted counselor or clergy.

Case Study

Fran was ten years younger than her spouse. She had been married to Tom for 30 years, and they had four children. Tom began complaining of feeling tired all the time and experienced numbness in his arms. One day, as Tom was mowing the grass, he felt a stabbing pain in his chest and experienced trouble breathing. Tom was having a massive heart attack. After months of rehab, he recovered, but his life was never the same. He did not have the energy to return to work and he tired easily.

Tom's health became an obstacle in his relationship with his wife. Fran worried that Tom might have a second heart attack. Intimacy was a big issue. Their children were independent and had children of their own. Her job as a consultant for a major corporation included some travel, but she experienced deep feelings of loneliness traveling on her own. Tom and Fran had counted on this stage of their lives to be their time for travel and fun together.

When Fran met Dave, who worked for one of her clients, she was very attracted to him. Dave had been divorced for eight years so he was ready for a love interest. Dave lived in another town so he and Fran could discretely meet anytime without Tom ever knowing. What happened to loyalty and trust in Tom and Fran's relationship?

Honesty

Honesty is another basic quality of a healthy relationship. It goes along with trust. Secrets drive a wedge in a marriage. Honesty creates an atmosphere in which it is safe to share who you are and to be yourself.

It's important for couples to be honest about their ideas about intimacy. In his book *The Five Love Languages,* Gary Chapman identifies five important ways for partners to relate to one another emotionally. For instance, women usually like to feel closer to their husbands by touching, hand holding, or hugging, whereas men like verbal support to reinforce how well they are performing their jobs or acting in the relationship. You may have your own preferred way of how you want and need your partner to relate to you and make you feel special.

When Claire was growing up, her family did not verbally express their feelings, but rather expressed love through all that they did for one another. So Claire never learned to express her feelings towards her husband with words. To Claire, it was enough to show her love by taking care of the household, the children, cooking meals, etc. Claire worked hard at maintaining their home and thought that John would notice and appreciate her spending time to make them comfortable. She wanted their home to be a place that he would look forward to returning at the end of each day, a place where she thought he felt nurtured and loved.

Responsibility

When two people decide that they care about each other enough to be in a relationship, what is the nature of that commitment? One very important feature is knowing whether your partner is responsible. Responsibility in a healthy relationship means that you are both accountable to one another for the success of the relationship. You agree to be dependable when assuming obligations and duties in a healthy relationship.

The following is a checklist to determine your degree of responsibility:

- Do you both make decisions about the relationship together?
- Is there a fair distribution of chores?
- Does your partner respect your right to make decisions about your own life?
- Does your partner give you emotional support?
- Does your partner respect your ideas and feelings as real?
- Is your partner willing to share information about his or her thoughts and feelings?
- Does your partner really listen to what you have to say?
- Do you both take enough time for the relationship?
- Do you and your partner fight fair?
- Do you mutually take care of one another's needs?

Good Communication

Being willing to talk to one another and try to understand what the other person is saying is critical to a healthy relationship. All of us have individualized styles of expressing our thoughts and feelings. As we receive information, we each have our own methods of processing what another person has said. Like the game "telephone" some of us used to play when we were younger, we may incorrectly interpret that information. Although the original message may have been, "School is out early today," someone may have heard, "The pool is murky today."

Often couples hear and interpret messages from their partners in a different way, and they experience a total disconnect. Neither one has an accurate idea of what the other is saying. They internalize false perceptions of the messages their partners communicated.

If you and your new partner have lots of misunderstandings, you may want to make an extra effort to communicate more clearly. When you are having a conversation, listen intently and then clarify that you have gotten the message correctly by summing up the key points and asking your partner, "Is this what you are saying?" Keep asking until you totally understand the points that your partner is making. Then it is your turn. Let your partner know if you agree or disagree with any of the points that have been made. Your partner then asks you, "Is this what you are saying?" and keeps asking you to clarify your points. This skill takes practice, but it does establish clearer communication.

Also good eye contact is important. Avoid multitasking while your partner is talking to you.

Unselfishness

When both members of the couple forget about themselves and try to make the other happy, the relationship is usually a caring, loving, fulfilling one. Here are some characteristics of an unselfish partner:

- Is sensitive to your feelings
- Respects your ideas

- Does things to make you happy
- Values your ideas
- Lets you be the special person that you are
- Is willing to listen to your side of the story on issues

Separate Identities

A healthy relationship stimulates both individuals' growth. Each person is encouraged to thrive and grow. A healthy relationship encourages personal development. Even though you are in a committed relationship, it is important to maintain your own identity. This means not giving up who you are just to be with that other person. People who try to please others all the time just to be accepted are known as codependent. Codependent people often exhibit their people-pleasing behavior with friends and family members as well as with their partner. Their self-esteem is so low that they don't realize that they can be accepted for who they are.

There are several clues indicating if both partners are maintaining their identity:

- Both individuals are allowed to fulfill their own needs and wants
- Both individuals encourage one another to find new interests
- Neither partner is intimidated or jealous by the other's new interest or hobby

Case Study

Gwen was very talented at arranging flowers. Along with her friend, Sally, who worked as her assistant, Gwen provided many arrangements for her friends' dinner parties, church activities, and weddings. She had always had a secret desire to own a small business. Earning money from this hobby that brought her so much enjoyment was her dream.

Gwen had never taken time to pursue her dream until her husband, Frank, retired.

When their children were grown, Gwen had more time to devote to developing her business. When she approached Frank with her idea he was very supportive. Gwen asked Sally if she would like to be her business partner. Sally accepted. Now Gwen and Sally have more orders than they can fill. Frank often helps Gwen deliver her beautiful creations and attends some of the parties and weddings as well. Gwen's dream came true and she feels truly fulfilled.

Sexual Compatibility

There are few areas that can cause such hurt or embarrassment as discussing expectations about sex. Being open and respectful about our sexual preferences, how we are touched, how we are respected, and what we need in order to make us feel fulfilled is an important part of a healthy relationship. Sometimes partners can verbally communicate how they want their lovemaking to transpire, but others are too shy or afraid they might offend their lover to state what they need in order to feel truly valued and loved in the relationship.

Many couples find it a challenge to communicate about sex openly and clearly. They may feel very vulnerable when discussing what would make them happy, or even fear rejection. Couples can become even closer if they are willing to tackle this sensitive subject.

Case Study

Sandy and Jack were in love and agreed on an exclusive relationship. Sandy moved in with Jack after they had been together for about one year. They planned to get married after they had saved enough money.

Jack was a "type A" personality, always busy, with a high-pressure job. He expected sex every night. He became very angry when Sandy did not give in to his desires. Sandy was happy with sex twice a week, but she felt it was her duty to honor Jack's wishes. No matter how exhausted she was from her day, she tried to please her partner.

After months of pleasing Jack, she began to feel used and angry. She became irritable and sometimes wouldn't talk to Jack. Understandably, her behavior made Jack upset. Both individuals found it hard to talk with one another about their problems. Instead, they screamed at one another, and then would not talk to each another for several days. Realizing that their relationship was in jeopardy, they decided that they had to talk.

Sandy told Jack that the nights that she came home tired from work, she would rather just cuddle. Jack needed to understand how tired Sandy had become, and that she was not being unreasonable. After much thought, Jack agreed that their pattern of making love needed to change and rather than losing her, he was willing to compromise. He loved Sandy and it was important for both of them to respect one another and feel valued in the relationship.

Feeling safe is critical when discussing sexual issues with your lover. A healthy sex life is an intimate experience that helps a couple feel closer, satisfied, and valued. It is important that individuals not feel intimidated if their partners' desires are different from their own.

Sometimes couples need more knowledge about one another's bodies and how to make love. They don't know how to satisfy one another. One good resource is *The Joy of Sex: Fully Revised and Completely Updated for the 21st Century* by Dr. Alex Comfort. Another resource is *How to Really Love the*

One You're With by Larry James.

In the past there wasn't much research done in women's sexuality after the age of 45. It was assumed that along with the aging process of graying hair and gaining weight, women lost interest in sex. However, by midlife, when the children are out of the house, when the couple is more financially stable, and there is no fear of pregnancy, they are free to enjoy sex more.

Alan M. Altman, M.D., and therapist Laurie Ashner have written the book *Making Love the Way We Used To...Or Better*, which provides medical information and communication techniques for dealing with any sexual problems that may occur at midlife. Gail Sheehy writes in her book *Sex and the Seasoned Woman* that women don't have to be in their 20s and 30s to enjoy good sex. Sheehy states that women in their mid-40s, 50s, and 60s are at the peak of their sexual lives. She concludes menopause gives women a chance to rethink their lives, which can lead to change.

Case Study

Janice was a 60-year-old woman who had been married for 25 years. She and her husband divorced because they couldn't seem to stop fighting. Several years went by and she had two failed love relationships. The men she attracted did not match what Janice was searching for. One individual drank a lot and the other was much older.

After these two unhealthy experiences with men, she began to ask why relationships didn't work for her. She had trust issues with men and feared that once again she would attract men who were just not right for her. In therapy, Janice took a good look at herself and began to get her confidence back. She realized that this was the best time of her life. She valued the qualities that she had to offer in a relationship. Her self-esteem improved and she started believing that she could have a meaningful relationship. She also made a list of the qualities that she would like in her next love relationship.

Janice developed a positive attitude about her future and conquered her fears about being good enough. She realized she was free to be the woman she wanted to be. A few months later she met a man at a social event who was compatible with her in every way. They developed an exclusive relationship that was satisfying to both.

Modern Maturity, the magazine of AARP (formerly known as the American Association of Retired Persons), commissioned a study about the sexual attitudes and practices of Americans age 45 and older. In this study, called "Sex at Midlife and Beyond," researchers found that life after 40 can be a fulfilling period for romance. More older people were enjoying sex than had been previously thought.

Women today have many choices as to how to make their sex life fulfilling. If your experiences with men in your life have been disappointing, there is every reason to believe that your life can be different, no matter your age.

Part IV

Embracing Change

*"Limitations live
only in our minds.
But if we use our
imaginations, our possibilities
become limitless."*

Jamie Paolinetti

Change Is Good

As you discover who you are and as you begin to make changes in your life as a single person, realize that this is a process. Learning takes place as your new life unfolds. It may feel as if you take one step forward, and then two steps back, but with every step, a "new you" is emerging.

Try living by the OATS method. This acronym stands for:

- Objective
- Activities necessary to achieve your objective
- Time needed to complete your actions
- Schedule

Identify what you want to achieve: that's your objective. Then name the activities that you need in order to achieve your objective. Estimate the time you need to complete your actions. Make a schedule to help you stay on target.

An example would be Claire's search for new friends. She needed to go where there would be a selection of people, so she chose some activities to attend, such as church meetings, yoga class, or her daughter's PTA meetings. Each one of these activities took time, but Claire learned to allow enough time for each one. She kept a schedule to help her know how often she would participate in activities. This effort helped Claire meet new people and form lasting friendships.

Steps to a different YOU:

- Set goals
- Define the steps you'll need to take to realize your goals
- Be open to new experiences: different job, new friends, different type of living quarters (apartment, condo, house), advanced education
- Be determined and persistent
- Develop a sense of humor
- Take care of your health
- Nurture yourself each day: take a walk or watch a sunset
- Walk with the Divine (God) every day
- Believe that you will make it

You must keep on trying until you are comfortable with the new you. Don't let anything get in your way of creating a new life for yourself.

Life pushes us into circumstances. You may get sick, or divorced, or remarry, or even move to a more affluent neighborhood. Each different experience makes you a different person. You can become an active, conscious participant in the process of discovering who you are now, post-divorce.

Many times the only thing you need to change is your thoughts. An example is given below.

Case Study

Katherine and her husband Doug had been married for 30 years. Doug traveled during the week to different cities and abroad. When he got home on weekends he was content to watch ballgames on television.

Katherine had a full-time job and by the weekend she wanted to go out to dinner. Doug refused to go with her. He wanted home-cooked meals. Although Katherine preferred to eat healthy foods, her husband had always eaten gravies and sauces, lots of bacon and fatty meats, and creamy rich desserts, such as lemon meringue pie. So she prepared two different menus every time they ate a meal. Even when Katherine was working late he expected her to cook when she got home. He would not prepare anything for himself.

Katherine was pretty, intelligent, and drew people to her because of her warm personality. When Doug and Katherine did go out with their friends, he belittled her in front of them. Doug would listen intently to what everyone was saying and then throw in a hurtful remark.

Katherine and Doug also had a son who was home from the army, temporarily living with them. He was very responsible and picked up after himself, washed his own clothes, and helped Katherine around the house.

Katherine knew she was miserable but she thought it was her duty to be "a good wife." She had never thought that she deserved to be in a partnership, with Doug taking his share of the responsibility. Katherine needed to change her thinking about relationships and what is fair. After several years, she decided to move out of the house. She began pursuing her dreams and her life gained meaning and purpose.

The true secret of a changed life is a change in your mental attitude and this requires effort. If you had a mother and father that nurtured and supported you, it will not be as fearful for you to make changes in your life because you grew up with emotional security.

Remember, your brain can change as a result of mental training to alter the brain circuits. So your mental attitude or your will toward the new self that you are forming is very important. If you believe in yourself and think that you can make it in life, there is a better chance that you will succeed.

Ask for Divine guidance. Take time to breathe, and in the stillness you may discern the direction that you need to take.

Have faith. Resist being a "doing machine" who is busy, busy, busy. When your mind is not at rest, audibly repeat words like "tranquility" or "serenity" slowly several times and see if your mind doesn't begin to quiet down and you feel peaceful.

A saying that Claire's mother used to repeat when things weren't going well was "This too shall pass!" It usually does, but you have to do your part.

All that was lost is less than what Claire gained through belief in herself and perseverance in changing her thought pattern. Now Claire knows that anything is possible.

At the start of Claire's journey, she did not know who she was. Claire did not take ownership of her part in her broken marriage. Through the process of creating her new self and her new lifestyle, Claire looks at life differently now. She has changed a lot. She values her children, her family, and her close friendships more than ever. Claire seeks Divine guidance in everything that she does.

Reaching for Your New Life

As a counselor, I am dedicated to helping those who are ready to begin their transformational journey. I continue to offer my support with this book, in my private practice, on my website, and in groups and seminars.

Barbra Streisand was quoted as saying that "music is the connective tissue among souls." Her 1997 song recording, "At the Same Time," provides listeners with an opportunity to experience this magic for themselves.

Just like Claire's story, these powerful song lyrics by Anne Hampton Galloway communicate the experience of love that connects us again to the world.

Think of all the hearts beating in the world
at the same time,
Think of all the faces and the stories they could tell
at the same time,
Think of all the eyes, looking out into this world
trying to make some sense of what they see...
Just think of all the hands that will be reaching
for a dream
Think of all the dreams that could come true...

My wish for you is that your dreams will come true.

"The very least you can do in your life is to figure out what you hope for.
And the most you can do is live inside that hope.
Not admire it from a distance but live right in it,
under its roof."

Barbara Kingsolver

Appendix A

The Holmes-Rahe Life Stress Inventory: The Social Readjustment Scale

The values in the scale are just to show the relative impact of stressful events on our lives both in the way we perceive the events and the increased incidence of illness and death that occur during the following 12 months. Note that even positive events such as Christmas or vacations can be stressful.

Put a check beside the point value of each of these life events that has happened to you during the previous year.

Mean Value	Life Event
_____ 100	Death of spouse
_____ 73	Divorce
_____ 65	Marital separation from mate
_____ 63	Detention in jail or other institution
_____ 63	Death of a close family member
_____ 53	Major personal injury or illness
_____ 50	Marriage
_____ 47	Being fired at work
_____ 45	Marital reconciliation with mate
_____ 45	Retirement from work
_____ 44	Major change in the health or behavior of a family member
_____ 40	Pregnancy

_____	39	Sexual difficulties
_____	39	Gaining a new family member (birth, adoption, older adult moving in, etc.)
_____	39	Major business readjustment
_____	38	Major change in financial state (a lot worse or better off than usual)
_____	37	Death of a close friend
_____	36	Changing to a different line of work
_____	35	Major change in the number of arguments w/spouse (either a lot more or a lot fewer than usual regarding child rearing, personal habits)
_____	31	Taking on a mortgage (for home, business, etc.)
_____	30	Foreclosure on a mortgage or loan
_____	29	Major change in responsibilities at work (promotion, demotion, etc.)
_____	29	Son or daughter leaving home (marriage, attending college, joined military)
_____	29	In-law troubles
_____	28	Outstanding personal achievement
_____	26	Spouse beginning or ceasing work outside the home
_____	26	Beginning or ceasing formal schooling
_____	25	Major change in living condition (new home, remodeling, deterioration of neighborhood or home, etc.)
_____	24	Revision of personal habits (dress, manners, associations, quitting smoking)
_____	23	Troubles with the boss
_____	20	Major changes in working hours or conditions

_____	20	Changes in residence
_____	20	Changing to a new school
_____	19	Major change in church activity (a lot more or less than usual)
_____	18	Major change in social activities (clubs, movies, visiting, etc.)
_____	17	Taking on a loan (car, TV, freezer, etc.)
_____	16	Major change in sleeping habits (a lot more or a lot less than usual)
_____	15	Major change in number of family get-togethers (a lot more or a lot less than usual)
_____	15	Major change in eating habits (a lot more or less food intake, or very different meal hours or surroundings)
_____	13	Vacation
_____	12	Major holidays
_____	11	Minor violations of the law (traffic tickets, jaywalking, disturbing the peace, etc.)

Now, add up all the points you have to find your score.

150 points or less means a relatively low amount of life change and a low susceptibility to stress-induced health breakdown.

150 to 300 points implies about a 50 percent chance of a major health breakdown in the next two years.

300 points or more raises the odds to declining health about 8 percent, according to the Holmes-Rahe statistical prediction model.

Use your score as a guideline only.

Appendix B

Taking Stock of Your Stress:
Early Signs and Symptoms

Use this stress test as an educational tool to identify areas of your life in which you are experiencing more stress. It is divided into several categories: emotional, physical, social, spiritual, and work. The more checks that you put in a category, the higher your stress level.

Emotional Score
☐ Feeling irritable
☐ Feeling inadequate
☐ Having a tendency to cry easily
☐ Experiencing a loss of confidence
☐ Having a detached attitude
☐ Feeling stupid
☐ Feeling paranoid
☐ Constantly feeling rushed
☐ Having outbursts of temper
☐ Complaining
☐ Acting callous
☐ Feeling disillusioned
☐ Having a shortened attention span
☐ Feeling trapped and alone
☐ Feeling restless
☐ Feeling like a failure

- [ ] Feeling unappreciated
- [ ] Never feeling finished
- [ ] Feeling guilty
- [ ] Feeling bored
- [ ] Feeling worried
- [ ] Feeling scared
- [ ] Being abrupt with people
- [ ] Feeling helpless
- [ ] Feeling impatient most of the time
- [ ] Experiencing recurring anger

Physical Score

- [ ] Having a tense feeling
- [ ] Having headaches
- [ ] Having insomnia
- [ ] Experiencing shallow breathing
- [ ] Having frequent colds
- [ ] Being overweight
- [ ] Being out of shape
- [ ] Having general aches and pains
- [ ] Feeling exhausted
- [ ] Experiencing hyperventilation
- [ ] Experiencing dizziness
- [ ] Having stomach distress
- [ ] Looking tired and washed out
- [ ] Having heart problems
- [ ] Biting nails
- [ ] Feeling stiff
- [ ] Feeling run-down
- [ ] Oversleeping
- [ ] Lacking energy

❏ Drinking too much

Social Score
❏ Forgetting to smile
❏ Being preoccupied with work when off duty
❏ Curtailing outside activities
❏ Having a change of personality for the worse
❏ Losing interest in activities once enjoyed
❏ Avoiding people
❏ Feeling distracted and detached
❏ Reneging on commitments
❏ Being unable to make decisions
❏ Feeling no sense of belonging
❏ Being unable to take a joke or be teased by others
❏ Seeing anything as too much effort
❏ Making critical judgments of yourself and others
❏ Taking yourself too seriously
❏ Not initiating social time with friends

Spiritual Score
❏ Feeling unloved
❏ Feeling isolated
❏ Feeling unable to commit
❏ Feeling cynical about life
❏ Feeling unwilling to take a risk
❏ Feeling no sense of purpose
❏ Questioning your faith
❏ Feeling cautious
❏ Feeling a loss of imagination
❏ Feeling unenthusiastic
❏ Having no vision for the future

❐ Feeling fear
❐ Feeling suspicious
❐ Feeling selfish
❐ Feeling you are pushing through life

Work Score
❐ Living for the weekend or days off
❐ Increasing absenteeism
❐ Feeling inflexible in the face of change
❐ Making a big deal out of small things
❐ Having difficulty saying no
❐ Having difficulty making decisions
❐ Making excuses
❐ Being late for work or meetings
❐ Forgetting things
❐ Blaming others or finger pointing
❐ Taking longer and longer to get things done
❐ Having difficulty saying yes
❐ Not trusting your judgment
❐ Feeling performance is never good enough
❐ Venting frustration on family/coworkers
❐ Making mistakes
❐ Having difficulty receiving criticism
❐ Procrastinating
❐ Being unable to see alternatives in the face of problems
❐ Avoiding certain tasks

Add up the number of checks to find your score. If you have several checks under one or more categories, don't ignore these signs and symptoms. Take steps to get your life under control.

Appendix C

Personality Traits of the Stress-Prone Individual

Listed below are ten personality traits of the stress-prone individual. Rate yourself from 1 to 6 according to how often you experience that trait yourself. Circle the number that best fits you.

A tendency to overplan each day
          Seldom 1   2   3   4   5   6   Often

Multiple thoughts and actions while involved in one activity
          Seldom 1   2   3   4   5   6   Often

Need to win—excessive competitive drive
          Seldom 1   2   3   4   5   6   Often

Persistent desire for recognition
          Seldom 1   2   3   4   5   6   Often

Inability to relax without feeling guilty
          Seldom 1   2   3   4   5   6   Often

Often impatient with delays or interruptions—want to hurry events
          Seldom 1   2   3   4   5   6   Often

Involvement in multiple activities and projects
      Seldom 1   2   3   4   5   6   Often

Set up deadlines and pressures for self
      Seldom 1   2   3   4   5   6   Often

Deny having limits to self and others
      Seldom 1   2   3   4   5   6   Often

Feel compelled to overwork
      Seldom 1   2   3   4   5   6   Often

In reviewing each of the above statements, underline the number that reflects where you would like to be in relation to this trait.

Appendix D

If you would like to know your personality type, go to the following website:

http://www.humanmetrics.com/cgi-win/Jtypes2.asp

Appendix E

How to Find Your Target Heart Rate

In order to get the most out of an aerobic workout, you should achieve your Target Heart Rate and then maintain it for the duration of your workout, in order to achieve the maximum cardio benefit.

Karvonen Formula:

This method of calculating your target heart rate is based on your Maximum Heart Rate and your Resting Heart Rate (also known as your resting pulse).

To determine your Target Heart Rate, do this:

1. Take your resting pulse (Resting Heart Rate) by counting the number of beats for 1 minute. For example, your Resting Heart Rate is 60 beats per minute.

    Example: Resting Heart Rate = 60

2. Subtract your age from 220 to calculate your Maximum Heart Rate.

    (This example is for someone 45 years old.)
    (220) - (your age) = MaxHR
    Example: 220 - 45 = 175
    Maximum Heart Rate = 175

3. Subtract your Resting Heart Rate (60 beats per minute) from your Maximum Heart Rate.

> (Maximum Heart Rate) - (Resting Heart Rate) =
> "Heart Rate Reserve" value (or HRR)
> EXAMPLE: 175 - 60 = 115
> Heart Rate Reserve Value = 115

4. Multiply your HRR times 60 percent or 80 percent depending on the intensity of training you prefer. Working out while maintaining your target heart rate at 80 percent capacity would give you a more intense cardio workout.

> 115 x .6 = 69 (60% training percentage)
> 115 x .8 = 92 (80% training percentage)

5. Add your Resting Heart Rate value to get your Target Heart Rate, in beats per minute.

> 69 + 60 = 129
> 92 + 60 = 152

So, if you are 45 years old, your Target Heart Rate zone is 129 to 152 beats per minute.

You can also go online to find your target heart rate at: http://www.active.com/fitness/calculators/heartrate/

Just enter your age, level of exercise, and click "Calculate." The online calculator will report your Target Heart Rate Range automatically.

Appendix F

Stress Prevention

Score each item.

1 (strongly applies) to 5 (never applies)

_____1. I eat at least two balanced meals a day.

_____2. I sleep seven to eight hours a night.

_____3. I exercise 30 minutes at least three times a week.

_____4. I don't smoke.

_____5. I take fewer than four alcoholic drinks a week.

_____6. I am the appropriate weight for my height.

_____7. I am in good health.

_____8. I have income adequate to meet my expenses.

_____9. I regularly schedule leisure time.

_____10. I have a network of friends and acquaintances.

_____11. I have one or more friends to confide in.

_____12. I talk about my feelings when angry or worried.

_____13. I give and receive affection regularly.

_____14. I take time for myself daily.

_____15. I have a hobby.

_____16. I do something fun at least once a week.

_____17. I organize my time efficiently.

_____18. I drink fewer than two cups of caffeinated beverages daily.

_____19. I practice relaxation, deep breathing, or yoga.

_____20. I have regular conversations with the people I live with about daily living issues.

20-35 Low Vulnerability to Stress—Excellent self-care

35-45 Medium Vulnerability to Stress—Fair self-care

46-60 High Vulnerability to Stress—You are not taking care of yourself

61+ Very High Vulnerability to Stress—Watch for serious stress symptoms. If your stress is higher than you anticipated, consider taking better care of yourself.

Appendix G

Breathing Exercise

Take a moment for yourself. Lie on your back or sit in a comfortable position. If you choose to sit, keep your back straight and relax your neck and shoulders. Gently close your eyes.

Take a deep breath. Put your hand on your abdomen and gently bring your breath all the way down.

Feel it rise (or expand) as you breathe in and, conversely, fall or recede as you breathe out.

At this moment only YOU are important.

Focus on each breath as you inhale as well as on each time you exhale.

Imagine you are "riding the waves" of your own breathing as you follow each breath to its duration. As you breathe, relax and release any worries or cares.

At times intrusive thoughts may come into your psyche. Any thought that comes, acknowledge it and return your focus back to your belly and the feeling of your breath coming in and out.

Even if your mind keeps wandering off, just bring it back to your breath no matter what thoughts may come up.

Try doing this exercise just a couple of minutes a day and increase it two or three times a week and see if you feel calmer, more relaxed, and maybe even have more insight into your problems.

Appendix H

Listen to Your Heart Exercise

Place your hand over your heart and take several slow, deep breaths. In your mind's eye, go inside your heart. Think of someone you love.

Be careful with your heart and notice where, with what, and whom you feel:

- Open-hearted or closed-hearted
- Full-hearted or half-hearted
- Strong-hearted or weak-hearted
- Clear-hearted or confused

Notice any sense of a problem or issue that may come to you. Have a gentle attitude with yourself and go only where it feels safe for you.

Continue to be aware of your breathing. Notice what word, phrase, or image comes to mind.

Here are some questions that will help you get acquainted with your heart:

What does your heart need right now?

What about that issue makes sense?

Where in the body is it felt?

What color, size, or intensity is it?

What does it have to teach or tell you?

Is there something like it in your past?

Receive, breathe, and welcome what comes; offer gratitude to your heart.

Works Cited

Begley, Sharon. *Train Your Mind, Change Your Brain: How a New Science Reveals Our Extraordinary Potential to Transform Ourselves.* New York: Ballantine Books, 2007: 9-11.

Bosch, Geraldine and Kim Bushaw. *Talking to Children about Divorce: Ages and Stages.* http://www.ag.ndsu.edu/pubs/yf/famsci/fs442w.htm, 1995.

Chapman, Gary, *The Five Love Languages.* Chicago: Northfield Publishing, 2004: 15.

Divorcesource. *The Parent/Child Psychological Evaluation. Divorce Checklists: Child Behavior.* http://www.divorcesource.com/info/checklists/childbehavior.shtml.

Douillard, John. *Mind, Body, and Sport: The Mind-Body Guide to Lifelong Health, Fitness, and Your Personal Best.* New York: Three Rivers Press, 2001: 33-53.

Fisher, Helen. *Why We Love: The Nature and Chemistry of Romantic Love.* New York: Henry Holt & Co., 2004: 182-188.

Holmes, Thomas and Richard Rahe. "The Social Readjustment Rating Scale." *Journal of Psychosomatic Research*, (Vol. II), 1967: 213-218.

Jung, Carl Gustav (August 1, 1971). "Psychological Types." *Collected Works of C.G. Jung, Volume 6*, Princeton University Press.

Kabat-Zinn, Jon. *Full Catastrophe Living: Using the Wisdom of Your Body and Mind to Face Stress, Pain, and Illness*. New York: Dell, 1990: 31-46.

Karvonen, M. J., E. Kentala, and O. Mustala. "The Effects of Training on Heart Rate: A Longitudinal Study." Ann Med Exper Fenn, 1957; (35) 3:307-315.

Kubler-Ross, Elizabeth and David Kessler. *On Grief and Grieving: Finding the Meaning of Grief through the Five Stages of Loss*. New York: Simon and Schuster, 2007: 7-24.

Lorenz, Konrad. *On Aggression*. Orlando: Harcourt Brace & Co., 1966: 145-152.

Ogden, Gina. *The Heart and Soul of Sex: Making the ISIS Connection*. Boston: Trumpeter Books, Shambhala Publications, 2006: 54-69.

Roizen, Michael F., M.D., and Mehmet Oz, M.D. *YOU: Staying Young: The Owner's Manual for Extending Your Warranty*. New York: Simon and Schuster, 2007: 77-84.

Rumi, Jalal Al-Din, and Coleman Barks. *The Essential Rumi*. New York: Harper Collins, 1995: 109.

Schaeffer, Brenda. *Is It Love or Is It Addiction?*, 2nd ed. Center City: Hazelden, 1997: 6-10, 143-147.

Works Cited

Sheehy, Gail. *Sex and the Seasoned Woman: Pursuing the Passionate Life.* New York: Random House, 2006: 6-7, 16-20, 26-45.

The National Coalition Against Domestic Violence. http://www.ncadv.org.

Triere, Lynette and Richard Peacock. *Learning to Leave: A Woman's Guide,* rev. ed. New York: Warner Books, 1993: 169-170, 194.

Welsh, Amanda. *The Identity Theft Protection Guide.* New York: St. Martin's Griffin, 2004: 14-16.

Recommended Resources

Marriage

Abrahms-Spring, Janis. *After the Affair: Healing the Pain and Rebuilding the Trust When a Partner Has Been Unfaithful.* New York: Harper Collins, 1998.

Anderson, Nancy. *Avoiding the Greener Grass Syndrome: How to Grow Affair Proof Hedges Around Your Marriage.* Grand Rapids: Kregel, 2004.

Gottman, John M. and Nan Silver. *The Seven Principles for Making Marriage Work.* New York: Three Rivers Press, 1999.

McGraw, Phillip. *Relationship Rescue: A Seven Step Strategy for Reconnecting With Your Partner.* New York: Hyperion, 2000.

Subotnik, Rona B. and Gloria Harris. *Surviving Infidelity: Making Decisions, Recovering from the Pain.* Avon: Adams Media, 2005.

Divorce

Ford, Debbie. *Spiritual Divorce: Divorce as a Catalyst for an Extraordinary Life.* New York: Harper Collins, 2001.

Smoke, Jim. *Growing Through Divorce*. Eugene: Harvest House, 2007.

Kids and Divorce

Brown, Laurene. *Dinosours Divorce*. Boston: Atlantic Monthly Press, 1986.

Emery, Robert, *The Truth about Children and Divorce: Dealing with Emotions So You and Your Children Can Thrive*. New York: Viking Penguin, 2004.
Author's note: This book shows the child's side of things based on controlled studies of children and divorce.

Garon, Risa J. and Barbara Mandell. *Talking to Your Children about Separation and Divorce: A Handbook for Parents*. Columbia, MD: The Children of Separation and Divorce Center, 1999.
Author's note: Good suggestions for parents about how to deal with divorce with kids.

Hunt, Elwell. *Keeping Your Life Together when Your Parents Pull Apart: A Teen's Guide to Surviving Divorce*. Columbia, MD: The Children of Separation and Divorce Center, 2000.
Author's note: Stories of two teens dealing with the break-up of their families.

Krementz, Jill. *How It Feels When Parents Divorce*. New York: Alfred Knoft, Inc, 1988.
Author's note: Children ages 7 to 16 share their feelings about divorce.

Long, Nicholas and Tex Forehand. *Making Divorce Easier on Your Child: 50 Effective Ways to Help Children Adjust.* New York: McGraw Hill, 2002.
Author's note: Concrete common sense ideas for parents about divorce.

Stern, Zoe and Evan Stern. *Divorce is Not the End of the World: Zoe and Evan's Coping Guide for Kids.* Berkeley: Tricycle Press, 2008.
Author's note: Written by kids, for nine- to twelve-year-olds.

Relationships

Lerner, Harriet Goldhor. *The Dance of Anger: A Woman's Guide to Changing the Pattern of Intimate Relationships.* New York: HarperCollins, 1997.

Jones, Laurie Beth. *The Path: Creating Your Mission Statement for Work and Life.* New York: Hyperion, 1998.

McClary, Cheryl. *The Commitment Chronicles.* Naperville: Sourcebooks, 2006.

Woititz, Janet G. *Struggle for Intimacy.* Deerfield Beach: Health Communications, Inc., 1995.

Christian Couples

McGee, Robert S. *The Search for Significance.* Nashville: W. Publishing Group, 1998.

McGee, Robert S. *The Search for Significance Workbook: Building Your Self-Worth on God's Track*. Nashville: W. Publishing Group, 2004.

Unhealthy Relationships

Berry, D. B. *Domestic Violence Sourcebook*. Los Angeles: RGA Publishing Groups, Inc., 2000.

Hague, Gill, Amy Mullender, and Rosemary Aris. *Is Anyone Listening?: Accountability and Women Survivors of Domestic Violence*. New York: Routledge, 2003.

Norwood, Robin. *Women Who Love Too Much*. New York: Pocket Books, 2008.

Peabody, Susan. *Addiction to Love: Overcoming Obsession and Dependency in Relationships*. Berkeley: Ten Speed Press/ Celestial Arts, 2005.

Schaeffer, Brenda. *Is It Love or Is It Addiction?*, 2nd ed. Center City: Hazelden, 1997.

Healthy Relationships

Altman, Alan, M. and Laurie Ashner. *Making Love the Way We Used to...or Better: Secrets to Satisfying Midlife Sexuality*. Chicago: Contemporary Books, 2001.

Chapman, Gary. *The Five Love Languages*. Chicago:

Northfield Publishing, 2004.

Comfort, Alex. *The Joy of Sex: Fully Revised & Completely Updated for the 21st Century*. New York: Crown Publishers, 2002.

Harrar, Sari and Rita DeMaria. *The Seven Stages of Marriage: Laughter, Intimacy and Passion Today, Tomorrow, Forever*. Pleasantville: Reader's Digest, 2007.

Jacoby, Susan. "Great Sex." *AARP/Modern Maturity*, September-October, 1999.

Katherine, Anne. *Boundaries: Where You End and I Begin*. New York: MJF Books, 1991.

Schechter, S. and A.R. Jones, *When Love Goes Wrong: What to Do When You Can't Do Anything Right*. New York: Perennial Publishing, 1993.

Sheehy, Gail, *Sex and the Seasoned Woman: Pursuing the Passionate Life*. New York: Random House, 2006.

Stress

Kabat-Zinn, Jon. *Full Catastrophe Living: Using the Wisdom of Your Body and Mind to Face Stress, Pain, and Illness*. New York: Dell, 1990.

Klein, Allen. *The Healing Power of Humor: Techniques for Getting through Loss, Setbacks, Upsets, Disappointments,*

Difficulties, Trials, Tribulations, and All That Not-So-Funny Stuff. New York: Penguin Putnam, 1989.

Rumi, Jalal Al-Din, Michael Green, and Coleman Barks. *The Illuminated Rumi.* New York: Dell, 1997.

Science

Begley, Sharon. *Train Your Mind, Change Your Brain: How a New Science Reveals Our Extraordinary Potential to Transform Ourselves.* New York: Ballantine, 2007.

Braden, Gregg. *The Spontaneous Healing of Belief: Shattering The Paradigm of False Limits.* Carlsbad, CA: Hay House, 2008.

Lipton, Bruce. *The Biology of Belief: Unleashing the Power of Consciousness, Matter and Miracles.* Carlsbad, CA: Hay House, 2008.

Middendorf, Ilse, *The Perceptible Breath: A Breathing Science.* Paderborn, Germany: Junfermann-Verlag, 1990.

Protection

De Becker, Gavin. *The Gift of Fear: Survival Signals That Protect Us From Violence.* New York: Dell, 1997.

Welsh, Amanda. *The Identity Theft Protection Guide.* New York: St. Martin's Griffin, 2004.

Career

Bolles, Richard Nelson. *What Color Is Your Parachute?* Berkeley: Ten Speed Press, 2008.

Bolles, Richard and Mark E. Nelson. *Job-Hunting on the Internet: A Desktop Companion to the Website,* 2nd, ed. Berkeley: Ten Speed Press, 2005.

Cameron Julia. *The Artist's Way: A Spiritual Path to Higher Creativity.* New York: Penguin Putnam, 2002.

Sher, Barbara. *I Could Do Anything If I Only Knew What It Was: How To Discover What You Really Want and How To Get It.* New York: Dell, 1994.

Health

Naparstek, Belleruth. *Staying Well with Guided Imagery.* New York: Warner Books, 1994.

Northrup, Christiane, M.D. *Women's Bodies, Women's Wisdom.* New York: Bantam Books, 2006.

Roisen, M. and Mehmet Oz. *You Staying Young.* New York: Free Press, 2007.

Seligman, Martin. *Learned Optimism: How to Change Your Mind and Your Life.* New York: Bantam, 2006.

Grief

Kubler-Ross, Elizabeth and David Kessler. *On Grief and Grieving: Finding the Meaning of Grief through the Five Stages of Loss.* New York: Simon and Schuster, 2007.

Westberg, Granger E. *Good Grief.* Minneapolis: Fortress Press, 2004.

Healthy Women

Braiker, H. B. *The Type E* Woman: How To Overcome the Stress of Being Everything to Everybody.* New York: Signet Books, 2002.

Helpful Websites

www.uptoparents.org
www.couplesinstitute.com
www.gottmaninstitute.com
www.couplesjourney.com
www.livereal.com

Relaxing CDs for Adults

Title	Artist
Comfort Zone *Spectrum Suite* *Sleep Soundly*	Stephen Halpern
Quiet Music	Steve Roach
The Pachebel Canon *with Ocean Sounds*	Anastasi Mavrides
Healing Dreams	Dean Evenson
Liquid Mind #2 *For Yoga and Massage*	Liquid Mind
Canyon Trilogy: *Native American* *Flute Music* *Earth Spirit*	Carlos Nakai
The Silent Path	Robert Coxon
Any Relaxation Tapes for Health	Belleruth Naparstek

Relaxing CDs for Children

Title	Artist
When You Wish *Upon a Star*	Daniel Kobialka
The Mozart Effect: *Music for Babies, Vol. 1:* *Playtime to Sleepytime*	Wolfgang Mozart
The Mozart Effect: *Music for Babies, Vol. 2:* *Nighty Night*	Wolfgang Mozart

About The Author

Sara Rose has a doctoral degree in psychology and is a National Board Certified Counselor. She is an experienced psychotherapist who works with clients on a variety of issues. Relationship issues and working with couples are a focus of her practice. She uses a variety of techniques blending cognitive behavioral therapy, Western psychology, and bodywork.

Dr. Sara lives in Charlotte, North Carolina, the proud mother of two grown children, and is a divorce survivor herself. The theme of her work is supporting and empowering individuals during their transformation to a new, healthier life. The courageous individuals she has been privileged to work with in her private practice, as well as her own personal journey, inspired her to write this book. Through her writing Dr. Sara hopes to encourage and nurture individuals as they navigate their life's journey.

Visit Dr. Sara at www.drsararose.com and join the conversation on her website and blog. If you are interested in hiring Dr. Sara for speaking engagements, workshops, or consultations you may contact her at:

email: sara@drsararose.com
website: http://www.drsararose.com
office: 704-525-1213

Dr. Sara Rose
P.O. Box 11892
Charlotte, NC 28220

LaVergne, TN USA
29 March 2010
177500LV00002B/2/P